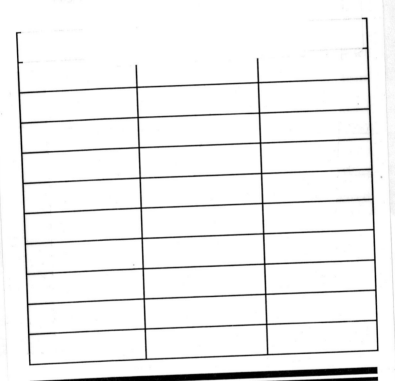

For my parents

DIVAS & DICTATORS

The Secret to Having a Much Better Behaved Child

CHARLIE TAYLOR

Vermilion
LONDON

3 5 7 9 10 8 6 4

Published in 2009 by Vermilion, an imprint of Ebury Publishing
A Random House Group Company

The Random House Group Limited Reg. No. 954009

Addresses for companies within the Random House Group
can be found at www.randomhouse.co.uk

A CIP catalogue record for this book is available from the British Library

The Random House Group Limited supports The Forest Stewardship
Council (FSC), the leading international forest certification organisation.
All our titles that are printed on Greenpeace approved FSC certified paper
carry the FSC logo. Our paper procurement policy can be found at
www.rbooks.co.uk/environment

Mixed Sources
Product group from well-managed
forests and other controlled sources
www.fsc.org Cert no. TT-COC-2139
© 1996 Forest Stewardship Council
FSC

Designed and set by seagulls.net

Printed in the UK by CPI Mackays, Chatham, ME5 8TD

ISBN 9780091923853

To buy books by your favourite authors and register for offers visit
www.rbooks.co.uk

contents

SECTION FOUR
Troubleshooting Guide

introduction

They throw tantrums over the smallest thing, they develop astonishing food fads that have their chefs running about in search of the correct ingredients, they demand continuous attention and can't bear it if anyone else gets a look-in, even for a moment. They leave their clothes and possessions discarded around the house and have no respect for other people's time or property. Ideally, they like to be followed around by a fawning entourage who will protect them from the outside world and bow to their every whim and command. They become self-centred and unpredictable, one minute they are charming and funny, the next they are screaming, crying delinquents.

Our children bring enormous happiness to our lives. However, at times, they may show the same impossible, irrational behaviour that we associate with grown-up divas and dictators from the gossip pages of newspapers and flickering black and white images on the History Channel. Parents, however calm and rational, have moments when the business of being a mother or a father gets too much. As a parent of three under-tens, I know how children have a remarkable, in-built capacity to push our buttons and a knack of doing it when we are at our most tired and stressed. Parents can easily get stuck in a cycle that begins to feed the bad behaviour and make it more likely to be repeated.

This book is for all parents, regardless of how well their children behave, not just for the few who put up with some really challenging behaviour. It is not about getting perfectly behaved children (what a hideous thought!), rather it gives a range of practical strategies that parents can use straight away to make their children's behaviour 'better'. As parents, we inevitably hit some sticky patches with our children. The ideas in *Divas & Dictators* will stop this behaviour developing into longer-lasting, more damaging patterns.

There is a lot of talk these days about the 'work-life balance' as though there is an achievable equilibrium when we achieve a nirvana of perfection as a parent, alongside a satisfying and stimulating career. The reality is that if we can find some sort of reasonable work/life muddle then we will be doing just fine. The strategies in this book will help make for calmer, more positive parents who feel less guilt and can spend more time enjoying the fun bits of bringing up children.

I developed the ideas in *Divas & Dictators* through my long experience of working with children with behavioural difficulties and their parents. I have taught for eighteen years in tough inner-city primary and comprehensive schools and I am currently the headteacher of a school for children with behavioural difficulties in west London. We take the most challenging and socially deprived children who have been excluded from school and aim to turn their behaviour round and get them back into mainstream education. I run regular training workshops for parents on positive behaviour management. I also do lots of work with individual parents who are having difficulty with their children.

This book contains a range of positive strategies that will give parents a framework to use when dealing with any type of behaviour. First, we look at why children misbehave and how the reactions of parents can feed into the pattern. Then I describe how, by dramatically increasing the amount of praise, parents can improve and embed better behaviour. There are additional sections on the role and effectiveness of rewards and punishments, on improving routines and a description of how to play with your children to get better behaviour. The last section of the book contains suggestions for dealing with specific, common issues that arise in all families, from bedtimes to car journeys to homework.

I hope that you will be able to read the book in full and then refer back to it whenever you need a bit of support, when some tricky behaviour arises.

I am acutely aware of the constant guilt we feel as parents that we are not doing as well as we should be. I hope this book will help you recognise what a good job you are doing. One of the overarching themes of the book is the use of praise and I wish, as parents, we were better at praising ourselves.

These strategies work with children with the most challenging behaviour at my school. They work with my own children. They will work with your children too.

the reptile brain

1

the reptile in us

Wild Threats or Bribes

The four-year-old starts screaming and throwing groceries out of the trolley, just as the baby is beginning to need a feed. The mother can feel her stress levels going through the roof and she has just noticed the disapproving stare of the woman behind her in the queue. She has stopped thinking rationally, she just wants to get home. To stop the child bawling the mother either gives a wild threat:

'Right! If you don't stop screaming then you can't watch any videos for the rest of the week.'

Or offers a bribe:

'Come on, darling, if you stop shouting you can choose a packet of sweets.'

When she gets home and calms down she realises that she needs her child to watch a video so she can bath the baby in peace. She also decides that the punishment she thought of in the heat of the moment was a bit too severe. Either she forgets about the threat completely, or she finds a way to get out of it.

'Right, you can watch a video tonight, but if you behave like that in the supermarket again, then you really won't be allowed to watch one next time.'

Or:

'As you've been so good since we got back, you can watch a video this time.'

Children soon learn to distinguish between a serious threat and a bluff and will treat each accordingly. If you listen to other parents (as well as to yourself) you will be amazed by how many empty threats you'll hear.

Bribes, on the other hand, will always work. Your child will quickly learn that a great way to get sweets is to throw a tantrum – the more intense, the more sweets. So starts a pattern that will get harder to break every time it is repeated.

It is easy to be critical of these two responses, but remember the parent is under stress and the adrenaline is flowing. The rational brain has shut down and they can't react logically or reasonably. They are 'in reptile'.

The Reptile Brain: Fight or Flight

When humans are faced with a perceived danger, the body begins to prepare itself to deal with the threat. This is known as the fight or flight reaction. The blood vessels in the arms and legs open up and blood is diverted away from the parts of the brain that deal with rational thought, to the muscles. The body is preparing to fight or run away. There is simply not enough blood to go round, and with less blood in the brain, the capacity to think clearly is reduced. This means that when humans lose their temper or are distressed they say and do things that they may later come to regret. The thinking part of the brain shuts down and we are left with the primeval part of our brain that is akin in complexity and understanding to that of a reptile. Under stress our brains work with all the judgement and rationality of an alligator.

The problem is that our body responds in the same way to an emotional threat as it does to a physical threat. If you worked on a checkout in a supermarket and you wanted to steal some money, you could short-change the customers with screaming children. They never check their change, and even if they tried they couldn't add it up – reptiles can't do maths.

Imagine trying to read a map ten minutes after you had been in a car crash. You would see the extent to which your rational brain had shut down.

In the following case study, when Maggie gets home and has to deal with a son who is trying to turn bedtime into a game, her body reacts as if she is being physically threatened. Our physical reaction to stress hormones is the same, no matter what has caused them to be released.

Bedtime in Maggie's House

Maggie has come back from a long day at work and she is feeling exhausted. She makes tea for her two children, Tom, five and Laura, two.

The trouble starts when she tells the children to go upstairs for a bath. Tom is in the middle of playing with his toy farm and completely ignores her. This ignoring thing from Tom has just started in the last week or so and Maggie is finding it really irritating. She calls him again and still he takes no notice. She has had enough so she leans over to him and shouts.

'TOM, BATHTIME.'

He gets up slowly and starts to go upstairs at zero miles an hour. Maggie grabs his hand and tries to speed him up; he thinks this is a game. He wriggles free and runs down the stairs again. Maggie goes after him, picks him up and carries him to the bathroom. Maggie gets Laura into the bath, but Tom refuses to get undressed and keeps running away. Maggie tries to jolly him along; she is feeling guilty after carrying him up the stairs.

'Tom, come on, darling, I've run a lovely bath.' He takes no notice and she gets really furious.

'RIGHT, NO BEDTIME STORY,' she shouts.

'I don't want a story tonight,' he says, running off.

'Okay, you're not going to the zoo with Daddy this weekend.'

Tom's face crumples and he starts howling. Maggie manages to get him undressed and into the bath. Laura is helped out and demands her milk. After her bedtime bottle, Maggie reads her a quick story. Meanwhile, Tom has been quietly tipping water on to the bathroom floor. Maggie really loses it.

'GET OUT NOW!' she screams and yanks him out

of the bath. 'Look at Laura, she's ready for bed already, why can't you be more like her? This happens every night, why can't you just do what you're told? Right! From now on we are going to have bathtime half an hour earlier!'

By pinning Tom down, Maggie gets him dry. He finally stops crying and puts his pyjamas on while she puts Laura to bed. Maggie comes back and they have a cuddle.

'I will read you a story tonight because you got dressed all by yourself,' she says.

They have an extra story, because Maggie is starting to feel really guilty about getting so angry. She puts him to bed and he promises to be good at bedtime the next day. Maggie goes downstairs and pours a glass of wine, and finally begins to relax after her day's work and the battle at bedtime.

Tom's bedroom door opens and she hears him padding down the stairs.

'Mum, I'm really hungry ...'

Any of that sound familiar?

Maggie came into the house feeling tense after her day at work. When she asked Tom to stop playing he ignored her twice, this tipped her over the edge and she began to lose her temper. She shouted at Tom, compared him unfavourably to his sister and made threats that she didn't follow through. Though she got her children to bed in the end, it was a traumatic experience all round and the chances are something similar will happen the next night.

Afterwards, Maggie felt guilty about what had happened, especially as she knew much of her anger was derived from tiredness due to her long day at work.

Maggie became angry and her body dumped a load of adrenaline into her bloodstream. This hormone produced the primeval reaction in her that helped to protect her ancestors from sabre-toothed tigers.

While Maggie's brain was short of blood she lost control of what she was saying and doing. As she started to calm down at the end of bedtime, the blood began to flow back to her brain and she was able to think more clearly. The guilt she felt meant she read Tom a bedtime story, even though she had told him she wouldn't. She also knew she wouldn't follow through with the threat to ban the zoo trip, either. The message this sent Tom was: *When I make a threat, don't take me seriously.*

It is also important to remember that children, as well as parents, go into reptile mode. Remember when someone shouted at you as a child, how you got frightened or angry? Those feelings cause the reptile effect in children, and like adults they can say and do things that they don't mean. Their capacity for rational thought and problem solving goes, and like their parents, they are unable to think straight.

Maggie decided that from now on she was going to start bathtime half an hour earlier. Not a bad idea in theory, but in reptile mode she has forgotten that they are out to tea for the next two days. They won't be back in time for the early bath and so the new plan will have to wait. Maggie has also forgotten that during the next week she has a couple of late meetings at work. The new regime hasn't been thought through and so it founders. This is hardly surprising, as it is impossible for anyone to start making plans when they are angry. Parents become hugely concerned about bad behaviour when it is happening, but they don't think about it when everything is running smoothly.

Unfortunately, it is while in reptile mode that we usually try and change our children's behaviour. We react by threatening dire punishments, shouting or, worse still, smacking. In addition, we often suddenly decide that there is going to be a new regime.

Right!

Whenever you find yourself starting a sentence like this, you can be fairly sure you are entering the realm of the reptile. It is supposed to sound strong and decisive, but what it usually means is, 'I've started to lose it.'

How Can I Stay Out of Reptile Mode?

Soldiers spend hours taking apart their guns and then putting them back together again. The process becomes second nature and they become so proficient that they can do it blindfolded.

Army training takes into account the flight or fight reaction and the loss of the rational brain under stress. When a gun jams on the battlefield the soldier can automatically strip the weapon down and correct the fault because he has rehearsed the procedure so many times. If he had to stop and think how to unjam a gun while the bullets were whizzing past his ear he would not be able to do it.

Under stress, humans don't function properly. Soldiers get round this by preparing in advance. I'm not saying there is a direct comparison between looking after children and going into battle, although some parents might think so. The point is this: if parents have a clearly thought out, well-rehearsed plan ready, when the trouble comes they will stay calm, stay positive and keep the reptile at bay.

The Reptile in Us: A Summary

1 When humans get angry, stressed or frightened, a physical reaction means their thinking brain stops working.

2 Parents in reptile mode make wild threats that they won't follow through or use bribes that encourage the bad behaviour to happen again.

3 If parents go into reptile, their children probably will too and things will start to get worse.

4 When parents come out of reptile, they often feel guilty and end up over-compensating. This teaches children not to take them seriously when they get angry.

5 The best way to avoid going into reptile mode is to make plans and be prepared for the trouble when it comes.

2

why do they do it?

Divas and Dictators are Nothing New

Go back twenty thousand years or so, and observe the nomadic family of primitive cavemen on the African savannah before you. It is time for them to move on, having stripped the surrounding area of roots and berries and frightened off all the deer. While the women and children gather up babies, animal skins, cooking-pots and some food for the journey, the men pick up their spears and start to look anxiously into the bush for sabre-tooth tigers and marauding mammoths. Suddenly, a four-year-old boy runs off, laughing, in the wrong direction. His mother puts down the baby she was carrying and runs after him. As she overtakes him, she clouts him round the ear and he begins to howl. His father comes over and tells him to shut up, but he carries on crying more and more loudly. The chief gives them a fierce scowl. The child puts out his arms to his father and says, 'Carry me,' in between loud sobs. The mother and father exchange looks, for the last time they had moved on they had agreed that the boy was too heavy to carry and that in future he was going to have to walk. However, the chief is now looking murderous, and the father can feel the irritation of the rest of the group, who have got their things together and want to move on. He bends over, picks up the child and hoists him on to his shoulders. The tribe moves off slowly. The father, feeling humiliated and fed up, takes it out on the boy's mother.

'Why did you let him run away in the first place?' he grunts.

'What do you mean? If you had taught him to do what he was told, we wouldn't have this problem.'

Up in his lofty position the child smiles broadly as he urges his father to go faster.

When they get to the new camping spot, the mother feeds her baby. As usual this enrages her son, who very gently bangs his knee on a rock and then reacts as if his leg is broken. His mother puts the baby down and comes running over to see if he is okay. She cuddles and reassures him until his father appears and offers to play a primitive version of football. The boy miraculously recovers, jumps up and demands that his father goes in goal.

His mother watches from a distance. 'Why is he so exhausting?' she thinks. 'Why can't he be easy-going like his little brother? *He* is never any trouble.'

Parents, inevitably, spend time comparing their children and trying to work out why, despite the similarity in upbringing, children seem to react totally differently to the same situation, and why one child behaves so much worse than another. There are many factors that can't be changed and one of the certainties is that some children will be trickier to manage and will test the boundaries more than others.

Attention

One of the prime, defining causes of all children's behaviour is the need for attention, as we saw with the caveman family. It is better to be noticed, clouted round the ear and carried than to be playing quietly under a tree and left behind. The need for recognition starts off at this very basic level: if you don't get noticed, then you won't get looked after or fed. For many animals, feeding and protection is all they require; instinct takes care of the rest. With our complex social structures and brains, humans have a lot more to learn from our parents and therefore need considerably more attention. Children need different levels and types of attention depending on their age and temperament. Babies need a huge amount of attention in the early months of life, to support both their physical and mental development. As babies grow into toddlers, they need less basic care, but continue to require enormous amounts of attention. As children grow up, the level of attention they require will change or even diminish, but the need for recognition from our parents will never go away. We can all think of adults who need a higher level of attention than the rest of us (or it might be you!). Children who don't get as much attention as they need will find a way to get it. Some children discover, subconsciously, that the fastest way to get attention is to do the wrong thing. We humans seem to be hard-wired to notice our children far more when they are misbehaving, than when they are doing what they are supposed to do.

At my school, we have some children who are so desperate for attention that they will go to any destructive length to get it. They have become utterly stuck in a negative-attention cycle and have a range of survival techniques, in which they are able to hook in the people around them in order to be noticed. One boy acquired the habit of provoking the biggest and most aggressive pupil in the school. He would sneak up behind him in the playground and push him over, or deliberately target him on the football pitch. The consequence was that he would get hurt, but the staff would have to intervene and he would be rescued and patched up by a first-aider. We were only able to break this cycle by giving him huge, over-the-top amounts of attention whenever he was being good and rewarding the bigger boy when he managed to ignore the provocation.

Children are simply trying to make sense of their world, and the way they behave is part of that process. Children learn that if they behave in a certain way, they can get adults to respond in a predictable way. If this response meets the child's need, whether the need is for attention or recognition, then the child will continue with the behaviour as long as the parent continues with the predictable response.

The New Baby

Tom is a six-year-old whose mother has just had a baby. As a result, she is not spending as much time with him as she used to. He feels insecure and craves his mother's love and attention. When he plays quietly with his toys, no one takes much notice of him because he appears to be happy. One day, he starts chucking his toys around. One of them lands near the cot, so his mother, naturally protective of her baby, storms over and holds on to his wrists, looks him in the eye and yells at him. Tom goes back to playing quietly and being ignored, but he has learnt a lesson, and it's not the one his mother tried to teach him. To get the attention he craves, he realises that the best thing he can do is to threaten the baby in some way. This will elicit a dramatic and instant response, in a way that playing nicely with his toys can never do. The attention he gets from his mother is negative and unsatisfying, but it's a lot better than nothing. A pattern now develops. Tom's need for recognition is sustained by being told off, but it is such an unsatisfying experience that he craves yet more attention. Depressingly, Tom's mother may also begin to harbour some resentment against him, which makes her less willing to engage positively with him. She may even start labelling him 'a difficult child' and comparing him: 'The baby's so easy, but Tom is a nightmare.'

Tom's world has been turned upside down by the arrival of the baby. He has developed a coping mechanism, but it is highly destructive. If this pattern were to continue unchecked, as it easily could, then Tom could enter a spiral of worsening behaviour that could begin to affect his schooling, his relationship with his mother and the development of his character.

The easiest way of gauging just how much of your child's behaviour is to do with a craving for attention is to give him lots and see what happens. Parents usually find that if they take one of their children off on their own, even the most difficult child will behave beautifully.

Every time parents are drawn in by and react to negative attention-seeking, they are making the behaviour more likely to occur again. Chapter 3 shows parents how to stay out of the negative attention-seeking pattern and stay positive.

Genes

The debate continues to rage as to how much of our personalities are inherited in our genes, but there is no doubt that genes play a role in the temperament of children. Some children seem to be born more difficult than others, screaming at the drop of a hat, never sleeping at the right times, feeding badly and rarely seeming settled or happy. As they grow up, these differences continue to show. It is usually only when parents have a second child that they see how different children can be temperamentally, despite a similar upbringing. Studies on identical twins show that some attributes, such as intelligence, seem to be more influenced by genes than others.

However, that is not to say because a child has inherited a certain temperament from his genes that his behaviour (good or bad) is set in stone and unchangeable. It is a cop-out for parents to simply say, 'That's just the way he is and we can't do anything about it.'

Early Childhood

If you stood outside a maternity hospital for an afternoon, you would be able to tell which number child was being taken home, just by watching each couple bringing the baby out and putting it into the car. The parents of a first child carry the baby like a priceless vase that could shatter with the slightest pressure. Watching them spend half an hour trying to get the straps in the right place in the baby-seat would be a bit of a giveaway, as would the way the non-driver sits, in full alert, on the back seat to keep watch. The parents of a second child come bouncing down the steps, holding the baby confidently and taking a second to strap him into his seat. The parents of a third child are the ones jauntily leaving the hospital, with the carrycot, the mother's suitcase, a few bunches of flowers, but without the baby – which they've forgotten to bring home.

When babies are born, the brain has not fully developed. It is continuing to 'wire-up' for the first few days, months and years, and this wiring-up process is affected by environmental factors. If the parent is unable to provide a loving and nurturing environment for the child during these early months, there is a strong likelihood that the child will develop behavioural, emotional and social difficulties later on in life. This was demonstrated with horrible force in the orphanages of Ceausescu's regime in Romania. Babies were placed in rows of cots, picked up only to be fed or changed and were given no stimulation or love. Scans showed later that there were actually physical gaps in the children's brains, especially in the areas which house emotion. The children whose cots were nearer the nursing station fared better, even with no direct attention, because just hearing the nurses' voices seemed to stimulate some brain activity. It comes as no surprise that babies who get lots of love and nurturing in the first months of life are more likely to become happier, and more stable, children and adults.

The Smiling Twins

Mona gives birth to non-identical, mixed-sex twins. At three months the girl, Dana, starts to smile. Mona, her husband John and all of the family smile back, which makes Dana smile even more. Whenever people come up to the cot and smile at the babies, Dana always smiles back, but the boy, Dominic, doesn't, because he hasn't learnt to yet. Everyone smiles at Dana, but they soon stop bothering with Dominic. Soon, the parents start to label Dana as the smiley one and Dominic as the miserable, grumpy one. Dominic starts to live up to expectations and finds other, less positive ways of getting attention. When the parents talk about the twins they say, 'Oh yes, Dana was always a really sunny, happy girl, even when she was a baby. But Dominic, he has always been difficult.'

This simple example shows how, inadvertently, parents can shape the personality of a child. What seems like temperament caused by genes is actually the result of the child's early experience.

Position in the Family

Oldest, middle, youngest or only? Just pause for a moment and consider how your position in your family has ruined your life. It is one of those unchangeable factors that has a huge impact on children. The oldest child, who gets the early attention from his inexperienced parents, is the trailblazer for his siblings. Oldest children often feel their parents are much stricter with them than with their younger siblings and they carry the weight of their parents' expectations. Oldest children are likely to be the most conventionally successful, entering the sorts of professions that their parents would want them to. The experiences of oldest children are often very similar, while the experiences of middle and youngest children tend to be more varied. The middle child can be the one who feels squeezed between his demanding siblings, or can be the lynchpin in the family who keeps everyone together. The youngest can be blessed and spoilt with attention by all the family, or an afterthought who never feels they quite get a look-in.

Position in the family is one of those factors that will inevitably have an effect on children's view of the world and their behaviour. It can't be changed, but it can be taken into account when trying to work out what is making your child tick.

Testing the Boundaries

As parents, we impose our values and beliefs on our children. We do this consciously, by telling and teaching them how we want them to behave, and subconsciously by our own behaviour, which they observe. From the age of three, children begin to develop their own values and beliefs. These originate from what they have learnt from us, but over time there is a subtle divergence between the values we want them to have and the ones they develop. One of the most important ways that children develop their own values is to test those that have been imposed by their parents. By challenging, they find out for themselves what is really important and this process feeds into the development of their own character. This divergence creates a tension that begins with toddlers and culminates in the parent–child conflicts that often characterise the teenage years.

Testing the boundaries is an important part of the process of growing up and it is both inevitable and healthy. It is therefore essential that children have boundaries in the first place. Parents who do not set boundaries are failing to give children a clear framework of values from which to learn and develop.

I have come across parents who don't set clear boundaries for their children, because they feel if they do, they will stifle the development of the child's character. This style of parenting often comes from parents who had a very strict and repressive upbringing themselves. More often, parents don't set clear boundaries because they are frightened of the consequences, for example a giant tantrum from their toddler. When parents are afraid to set boundaries, the consequence is that every decision the adult makes is open to negotiation. The children push continuously, because they have learnt that if they make enough of a fuss they will get their own way. The parent is left exhausted and drained by the whole process and the relationship between parent and child is constantly under strain.

The world can be a scary and unpredictable place for children. Boundaries help children to feel secure, because they feel the adult is in control and will look after and protect them. Remember, even if they don't like them (and they quite likely won't), children *need* boundaries to help them feel safe. If there are no clear boundaries, the result is often children who become very controlling in the home. These children try and impose their own boundaries, rules and constraints on the world around them, but because they are children they get it wrong and they create a self-centred dictatorship. Without parameters set by the parents, children will find it hard to fit into the real world, in which there are all sorts of social and legal constraints that have to be followed.

Why Do They Do It?: A Summary

1 Children's behaviour is a result of a combination of their genes and their environment.

2 There are aspects of a child's temperament that cannot be changed but these should not be used as an excuse for a child's behaviour.

3 All children need attention and any attention is better than nothing.

4 Children and parents can get into a pattern of negative attention-seeking.

5 Children need to test the boundaries.

6 Children will set their own, self-centred parameters if parents don't do it for them.

3

make a plan

Planning for Good Behaviour

Preparation is the key to avoiding damaging patterns developing. It is an uncomfortable truth for parents that the only way to change their children's behaviour is to change their own. When parents are confronted by bad behaviour, they often react in a way that makes things more likely to happen again and leaves them feeling inadequate and guilty. If, as the behaviour is happening, the parent goes into reptile mode, things will not change. Reptilian responses to bad behaviour tend to feed the pattern. However, if parents can learn to react in a positive, predictable and constructive way, I can assure you that the child's behaviour will change.

What Can Parents Do to Stop It Happening Next Time?

Most of the time, parents can predict which times of the day and under which circumstances there's going to be trouble. It may be bedtime, bathtime, getting dressed, getting undressed – the list is endless. Despite the predictability of these situations, parents tend to react rather than prepare. If, as a parent, you have ever found yourself trotting out expressions such as:

'Every time we come here this happens.'

'You always keep the family waiting in the morning.'

'You still can't get dressed by yourself and you're four years old,' then it's time to take a step back and make a plan.

With some thought, it is possible to be ready for most situations. The plan can be followed when things start to go wrong and the trouble can be short-circuited. If you don't make a plan, the alternative is to keep on reacting to your children's behaviour in the way you always have done. This will get you more of the same behaviour.

Making a Plan

The first thing to do is to think about the problem. This needs to be done when the children are not around and the parent is feeling calm. Trying to make a plan minutes before the moment of conflict is unlikely to succeed, as the adrenaline is already beginning to flow and the reptile brain is taking over.

Sit down, pour yourself a stiff drink and ask yourself the following questions:

- *What is the behaviour I want to stop?* It helps to be very specific about this. If there are lots of things, start with the one you think will be the easiest to change. Once you have got into the habit of making successful plans you will find changing the more challenging behaviour easier.

■ *When does it happen?* Consider who else is around at the time. Often the presence of siblings is a factor.

■ *How do I react to the behaviour?* Think about what you say and how you say it. Does your reaction make the situation better and less likely to happen again? Does the behaviour seem to happen more when you are tired? If so, then it might be your bedtime that needs to change.

■ *How much of the bad behaviour can I safely ignore?* Often simply ignoring behaviour will make it go away. It helps to work out your bottom line.

■ *What would I like to see instead?* Be precise and make sure you are being realistic.

■ *Look at other factors that may be contributing to the problem.* Is my child getting enough sleep? Is he hungry or thirsty?

■ *What reward could I use when I see the right behaviour?* See Section Three.

■ *What sanction could I use when things go wrong?* See Section Three.

Once you have made a plan, the next job is to teach it to your child. This should not be done at the last moment. Find a quiet time when any siblings are out of the way, or if necessary, stick them in front of a DVD or get a friend or partner to take them out.

1. Explain the problem to the child by simply describing what you see happening. Don't turn this into a telling-off or the child will start going into reptile mode and you need him to be thinking. 'When I ask you to come up for a bath you usually run away and I have to chase you round the house and I get cross.'

2. Explain how things are going to be in the future. Young children respond well if you make it sound exciting. 'Tonight we are going to try a new, special bedtime. When I call you for your bath, I want you to come straight away.'

3. Practise it a few times, giving loads of praise when they do it right. Children love rehearsals. 'Okay, let's pretend it's bathtime now and in a second I'm going to call you. When I do, you've got to come straight away. Do you think you can do that? You can? Okay, let's try it. Wow, you came the first time I called you. Well done! Shall we try it again?'

When selling a new idea to children, use lots of pantomime. Make it sound as though you are excited and enthused about the idea, and your child will be hooked in by your panto display. If you put as much time and effort into selling the idea as you would normally use for telling them off, then you will be on the right lines.

4. Explain the reward. 'Tonight, when I call you for bathtime, if you come straight away I will read you an extra story.'

5. Prepare the child. 'I'm going to call you for bathtime in a few minutes. Can you remember what you are going to do? And what's going to happen if you get it right? That's right, an extra story.' (More panto!)

6. Praise him as he starts to do it. 'Bathtime! Well done! You are coming when I asked you. You're going to get an extra story tonight. You did it!'

7. Repeat the process the next night, building on the success. 'You remember last night you came when I asked you and you got an extra story? Shall we see if we can do it again tonight?'

8. Stick with it. It takes time for the new behaviour to become embedded. Don't stop with the plan until you are sure you have cracked it. Don't be tempted to use the reward for other things. Keep the focus on the behaviour you want to change.

When you first start following a plan it can seem very contrived and unnatural. Some parents even say it feels manipulative, but actually you are just applying your intelligence to a problem. Once you have tried it a few times you will get used to the process and it will become second nature. You will find that making plans is effective in changing all kinds of behaviour from day-to-day problems to more serious situations. To see how planning ahead can work, look at this example of Rachel and her daughter, Kim.

Kim and Rachel Go to the Supermarket

'My four-year-old-daughter Kim loves coming to the supermarket with me. She gets very excited on the way, talking about all the things she's going to buy. She used to sit in the trolley and I could control her quite well, but now she insists on walking. She won't stay with me for long and likes to run up and down the aisles. I spend most of the time chasing after her and she thinks this is a great game. In the end I usually have to hold her firmly by the hand and half-walk, half-drag her round with me. She keeps grabbing things off the shelf and putting them in the trolley and she gets in a rage if I put anything back. When we get to the checkout, the trouble really starts. She demands sweets and starts pulling them off the rack. I try to grab them back off her, but she often runs away again. I have to stop loading the shopping bags up and go and find her. This is particularly embarrassing if a queue has formed behind me. The shopping trip ends in one of two ways. Sometimes I end up giving her a smack, picking her up and carrying her back to the car without the shopping, but usually I just give in and I buy her the sweets.'

Trips to the supermarket for Rachel have become a nightmare. When Kim begins to act up, Rachel becomes stressed and starts making reptile responses. A pattern of action and reaction has now been established in which mother and child both play out their parts.

Rachel's reaction to Kim's behaviour is crucial. When Kim pushes it a bit, Rachel stays in control, but when Kim really loses it, Rachel buys her sweets so that they can finish the shopping and get home. The message this sends is: *If you really go for it I will give in.* Rachel needs to make a plan and stick to it even if she's going to have the embarrassment of a screaming child on her hands. If Kim's father, Matt, and Rachel plan together and back each other up, things will change even more quickly.

Here is a plan for Rachel.

- *Tell Kim what is expected of her*
   'When we get to the supermarket you are going to stay close to me. I would like you to help me choose things and put them in the trolley, but if I decide to put anything back you must do it even if you don't want to.' Rachel should also ask Kim to repeat the plan back to her to ensure it has sunk in.

- *Offer a reward*
   'If you stay close to me and help me put things in the trolley, I will let you choose a sweet when we get back to the car.'

- *And a threat of a consequence*
  'If you can't do what I've asked then I will take you home and you won't be able to come to the supermarket with me or choose a sweet.' Seeing her mother leave for the supermarket without her will send a very strong message to Kim.

- *Prepare for success*
  Before they leave for the supermarket, Rachel should talk Kim through the plan. She should explain again what is expected of Kim and remind her of the reward if she follows the plan and the sanction if she doesn't.

- *Praise her*
  As she goes round the shop, Rachel needs to praise Kim for sticking to the plan, letting her know that her efforts are being noticed. The praise also serves to remind Kim what she should be doing. The best way to do this is to use a running commentary style of praising. 'You're staying very close, well done.' 'You're doing exactly what you said you would.' 'You put back those ice creams even though you wanted to keep them.' Rachel must praise Kim more times than she used to tell her off. When Rachel gets home, she can praise her to Matt as well, in front of Kim.

- *Keep to the deal*
  If Rachel promised a sweet as a reward then she must make sure Kim gets one. If Kim does especially

well, Rachel may be tempted to give her more than one sweet. This would be a mistake as the reward becomes devalued and Kim will expect it every time. If Kim has messed about, and Rachel has had to take her home, she shouldn't be tempted to let Kim have a sweet even if she screams the house down. If Rachel can follow through with her sanction, then Kim will begin to realise it is not worth making a fuss. Screaming won't get her anywhere.

■ *Don't give up*
It will take time for Kim to realise that her old way of behaving is not going to get the same results it used to. Things will probably work fine the first time, but when the novelty wears off, Kim will test Rachel out to see if she is really serious. To make the plan work, Rachel and Matt will need to back each other up when things go wrong.

After two weeks of sticking to this strategy, Rachel and Kim could shop together successfully. This calm, planned approach helped to improve things in the supermarket and it also gave the parents a model for sorting out other behavioural problems in the future.

What's the Difference Between a Bribe and a Reward?

A bribe is given to stop a child doing something bad they are doing or are about to do. A reward is given when a child does something positive that was agreed on in advance. Bribes are given by parents who are not in control to get the child to stop doing the wrong thing. Rewards are given by parents who are in control to encourage the child to do the right thing. The difference is subtle, but is of fundamental importance. Bribes encourage more bad behaviour; rewards encourage more good behaviour.

Make a Plan: A Summary

1 Planning means parents can respond calmly and predictably to conflict moments. The reptile is kept at bay.

2 Planning should be done when you are relaxed and the children aren't around.

3 Plans must be realistic. Don't make a plan you won't be able to stick to.

4 Keep trying. If you give up and go back to the old pattern the child won't take you seriously next time you try and change things.

5 Be sure to notice when things have changed and let the child know.

6 Praise more often than you used to criticise.

section two

the 6 to 1 strategy

4

what is the 6 to 1 strategy?

In the last section we saw how one of the fundamental reasons for children behaving badly is the need for attention. We will now look at how parents can use this need to get better behaviour.

The key to improving children's behaviour is praise. The more praise, the better the behaviour will become. Parents who give out the most praise have better behaved children than those who always look to criticise and correct bad behaviour. It seems like an enormous contradiction, but the worse the behaviour, the more praise is required. This chapter will show parents how increasing the right sort of praise will have a dramatic effect on their children. Ultimately, if parents are able to average six pieces of praise for every piece of criticism, they will quickly notice a change not only in their children, but also in themselves. I call this my 6 to 1 strategy.

If you recorded yourself interacting with your children, how would you sound? A lot of parents would be surprised by what they hear. There would be a barrage of instructions: 'Get dressed; finish your food; sit down; stand up; put your coat on; stop doing that ...' and so on. There would also be praise, especially if things were going well and the children were behaving themselves. If their behaviour was bad, you would hear more instructions and a lot more correcting, and the praise would probably all but disappear.

In my work supporting teachers I have spent many hours observing in classrooms. I used this simple tally to keep a record of praise and criticism in the classroom:

Positive comments	Negative comments
✔ ✔ ✔ ✔ ✔	✔ ✔

Some teachers gave out praise constantly, while others would only nag. One teacher gave out forty-seven pieces of criticism without once praising anyone in a half-hour lesson. Sadly, this was not unusual. What I quickly noticed was that the teachers who praised the most had the best-behaved classes. When teachers got the ratio of praise to criticism up to around 6 to 1, incidents of bad behaviour all but disappeared.

At first, I thought this was simply because these teachers had easier classes, until I tracked classes as they went from teacher to teacher throughout a school day. Quite simply, the higher the praise-to-criticism ratio, the better the behaviour. I then began recording teachers and getting them to tally their own praise-to-criticism ratios, setting them the target of getting up to 6 to 1. Those who managed to achieve it (and not everyone could, old habits die hard) saw a dramatic improvement in the behaviour of their classes.

Outside the classroom, in my work with parents, using the 6 to 1 strategy has the same effect. When parents are able to radically increase the amount of praise they give out, they will see a significant improvement in their children's behaviour. This is easy when the behaviour is good, but when the behaviour is bad it is really hard to keep the ratio up. It goes right against the grain to praise a child who seems hell-bent on annoying you.

How to Start Using 6 to 1

When children are noticed by their parents for doing the right thing, their behaviour will begin to improve. When the behaviour has become really challenging, parents have to make a conscious effort to notice and praise things the child is doing right. After all, if a child is hitting his sister every five minutes then there are four minutes and 59 seconds when he is not hitting her and can therefore be praised. Parents can easily get out of the habit of praising and forget the power of catching their children being good.

It's not easy. I use 6 to 1 with my own children and even though I know it works, when I'm tired or stressed or they are being particularly annoying, I often don't manage it. 6 to 1 is counter-intuitive; it takes practice and real commitment on the part of the parents. Catching children being good helps to change the currency of recognition in the home from negative to positive and will change children's behaviour. Remember, if a child is not misbehaving, then there will be something to praise. This focus on the positive will usually begin to take effect in a few days, though it may take slightly longer for children whose behaviour is more challenging. Don't forget that thanks to the reptile brain, it is impossible to start this new regime when you are in the middle of a battle. People who are stressed are not in a position to take on change. It is most effective to start in the morning and explain to the child the sorts of behaviour you are looking forward to noticing. This will help to set the tone for the new positive climate. It does sound a bit artificial at first, but it will soon become easier.

Victoria called me in despair about Sam, her five-year-old who had become very jealous of his younger brother, Joe. Whenever Joe started playing with a toy, Sam instantly decided he wanted to play with it too. He would reach over and grab it, often hurting his brother in the process. Victoria would shout at Sam, take the toy and give it back to Joe. By then Joe was usually in tears and ended up getting taken away for a cuddle. When he came back, Sam felt he had missed out on the attention, so he would start the process again. Things had got so bad that Victoria couldn't leave them in the same room together.

6 to 1 for an Attention-Seeker

Sam and Victoria were stuck in a negative cycle that was feeding Sam's poor behaviour. He had discovered that a sure-fire way of getting Victoria's attention was to wind his brother up. The problem was that the attention he was getting was short-term and negative, so his need for attention was only being met very superficially. Victoria also admitted that she was so fed up with him that she wasn't feeling inclined to play or read to him as much as she used to.

We sat down and made a plan to break the cycle.

First Victoria explained to Sam how she wanted him to play.

'Good morning, Sam. Today I'm going to be looking for you playing really gently with Joe. That means that even when he's annoying you have got to come and find me or look for something else to do. Do you think you can manage this?'

'Okay.'

'That's great news, thank you.'

Then Victoria made a point of praising Sam whenever she saw him playing or sharing with Joe.

'You are being so gentle, well done. It's great that you are sharing your toys so well with Joe. You were very careful when you borrowed that toy ...'

By letting Sam know what was expected of him and then leaping on any good behaviour with loads of praise, Victoria was able to change things around very quickly. Sam and Joe started to play together much more and Victoria spent far less time nagging or patching up rows.

This case study shows how lots of praise can sort out a situation that could have become long-term and damaging to family unity. With children under five, it is remarkable how quickly parents can change things simply by noticing what their child is doing right, rather than just picking on what they do wrong.

Where possible, parents should aim to ignore any low-level bad behaviour, but they should be still be prepared to step in to stop anything more serious. If you do have to reprimand your child, then be ready to catch him being good again as soon as possible afterwards. The aim is to teach the child that good behaviour will get your attention.

The following case study is from my time as a second-ary school teacher, and shows how powerful praise can be in changing behaviour, when it is used in the right way.

The Boy Who Couldn't be Praised

I spent three years working in a comprehensive school in central London with disaffected boys. They were in danger of permanent exclusion from school and were beginning to get acquainted with the criminal justice system. One of the most challenging was Dean. Dean was fourteen years old, tall and good-looking with floppy blond hair. He had immense charm, which he could turn on and off at will. The teachers couldn't stand him. Many of them had been beguiled by him and then, just when they thought he was on their side, he would let them down spectacularly and publicly. I saw this happen with a newly qualified science teacher. She was finding the class reasonably easy to control, largely because Dean, with his own peculiar combination of charm and menace, had decided to help her.

One morning the teacher decided the class was settled enough to do a chemistry experiment involving Bunsen burners and acids. Dean made the other children listen as she explained and then he helped her with the organisation. After twenty minutes, things were going very well by the standard of a Year Eight science lesson in that particular school, and the teacher decided to pop out to get some more equipment. In the seconds she was away, Dean unleashed hell. Persuading one of the less intelligent pupils to set fire to his exercise book, Dean grabbed hold of a fire extinguisher and let it off, firing white powder all over the boy and most of the rest of the class. When the teacher came back in, the class had flipped into hysteria, with children charging round the room, throwing equipment and screaming. In the mêlée, someone set the fire alarm off and the whole school had to troop out into the playground to answer the register. The teacher got hold of Dean and tried to ask him what had happened.

'You left the lesson, Miss, that wasn't safe. You are lucky I was around to put the fire out.'

She got him into her classroom, sat him down and tried to have an adult-to-adult conversation. After a minute, he got up and walked out.

'Sorry, Miss, it's my break time.'

Teachers are taught not to take things personally, but nothing gets to them more than thinking they have a relationship with a child who then turns on them. As a result, there was a campaign run by some of the teachers to exclude Dean from the school.

I was assigned Dean among a group of disaffected teenagers I had been asked to support. I knew him well by reputation and I had come across him before on the periphery of trouble around the school. Before I started working with Dean, I did some digging around in his files. He had had a very troubled upbringing and had spent three years with a range of foster carers when his mother's drinking had prevented her from being able to look after him and his sister. It seemed that Dean had never been controlled by his mother and so he was used to controlling things himself.

I vowed to myself that whatever Dean did, I wasn't going to let it get to me. Then I set about trying to build a relationship with him. I soon realised that his confidence was all bluff and that he had an incredibly low opinion of himself. This was compounded by the fact that he could hardly read or write. His experience of life had taught him to expect people to let him down or abandon him. As a result, he would get his *retaliation in first and push away anyone who tried to get close. I also realised that Dean could not accept a compliment. If I or anyone else said anything positive to him, he would become aggressive and would often walk out. He was comfortable with being shouted at or criticised, presumably because he felt he deserved it and had become used to it.*

My main aim was to teach Dean to take a compliment and I realised that the best way was to choose things he couldn't argue with or deny. So, whenever he was doing the right thing, I told him so, but I avoided using praise words like 'well done' or 'that was brilliant', as these produced his anti-praise reaction. Instead, I simply described what he was doing. 'Dean, you've picked up your pen.' 'You got down to work in fifteen seconds.' 'You answered me politely.' It was hard to do because as a teacher, saying 'well done' was ingrained, but Dean began to make progress. As he became more confident with me, I began to slip in the odd praise word and he began to accept them, but he would refuse any compliment given in public. I called a meeting of all the staff who worked with Dean and I explained what I had been doing with him. Virtually all of them wanted to complain about him and tell stories about what he had been up to. I explained that he liked to be praised, little and often, without hyperbole and only in private. Some of the teachers were too far down the line with Dean to try anything different, but some agreed to give it a go. Two weeks later, we met up again. Some of the most negative staff didn't show up, but of those who did, most had noticed an improvement. Teachers were popping over to his desk and having a quiet word in his ear, or keeping him back after a lesson to tell him the good things they had noticed.

There was a major setback when one of the teachers keen to get rid of him shouted at the top of her voice across a crowded playground: 'Mr Taylor, this boy hasn't changed at all!' while pointing aggressively at Dean. After this, he went back to the old way of doing things, he had taken a risk by behaving better and he had been publicly exposed. It was a revenge attack from the teacher for previous encounters with Dean and it showed the depth of feeling his behaviour had caused in otherwise decent staff. It took some time to get him back on track, but luckily he had enough positive experience in the bank to make it worth having another go. He made it through school when it had been almost inevitable that he would be excluded.

I asked Dean what reward he would like to earn if his behaviour improved. I assumed he would want a trip out to McDonald's or the cinema, or time on the computer or extra football, but he only wanted one thing: 'If I'm good, tell my mum.'

This story illustrates the intensity and power of children's need for praise and acceptance from their parents. It is a pervasive need that continues into adulthood and stays with us for the rest of our lives. How many things do you still do to please your mother and father?

With younger children, this desire is stronger and is less diluted by environmental or peer group factors. While older children (and adults) can often find it hard to accept praise, under-fives can't get enough. This need for recognition and praise is a powerful force that can be harnessed by parents to help their children to behave. Children who are not praised find their own negative ways of getting recognition.

What is the 6 to 1 Strategy?: A Summary

1 Using praise is the most effective way to improve or change behaviour.

2 The more children are praised, the better their behaviour will become.

3 Children do not behave badly all the time, even if it seems like it sometimes.

4 Whenever children are not behaving badly they must be doing something right. Catch them being good.

5 To change behaviour, parents should use a 6 to 1 praise-to-criticism ratio.

5

how to praise

I recently worked with Louise, a mother who had got into such a downward spiral with her five-year-old son Josh that she had completely lost the habit of praise. Louise would try to ignore his low-level attention-seeking – such as throwing his food around and jumping off the furniture – but he would push the boundaries until Louise had to do something about it. His favourite trick was to pretend to hurt himself and then scream until she came to his aid. She tried ignoring him, but Josh would sometimes be genuinely hurt and she would be left feeling guilty. Whenever Josh was behaving nicely, Louise took the opportunity to have some time to herself or make a phone call. Josh soon learnt that if he played quietly, his mother would ignore him, but if he feigned an injury he could always get her attention.

Praise is the most powerful tool that parents have for improving their children's behaviour. It carries far more weight than a telling-off, shouting or imposing sanctions. Indeed, most of the time, praise is the only thing needed to get children to behave. My objective with Louise was to help her to focus on those moments when he was playing well. She felt that if she interrupted these moments then the spell would somehow be broken and he would go back to attention-seeking. Louise had to learn to resist the temptation to ignore Josh when he was being good, and to jump in and praise him and sometimes even join in with his game.

Parents usually understand the importance of praise, especially with young children, but they don't always use it effectively. Often parents tell their children that they are 'wonderful, amazing, incredible, fantastic'. It was this type of praise that Dean couldn't cope with: he didn't believe it, because he knew it wasn't true. Hyperbole is positive and probably helps to raise self-esteem and it's a lot better than being critical. However, as a currency, this sort of praise soon gets devalued. Is a child really 'wonderful' if he manages to finish his lunch? Is it 'incredible' to get into bed on time? When a child receives this sort of praise he or she is left with a pleasant feeling that they have done something right, but they often don't know exactly what. This is especially confusing for children who have been misbehaving, but just haven't been caught. 'Darling! You're wonderful' ends up being interpreted as 'Congratulations! You got away with it!'

Descriptive Praise

If children don't know what they are being praised for, they won't know how to get a repeat dose. The object of praise is to help children feel good about themselves, but it is also a way of helping them to do the right thing next time. It is important to be explicit about what they did right. You don't even need to include praise words like 'good' or 'well done' – the description is often enough.

'You did your homework.'

'You shared your toys.'

'You got dressed by yourself.'

'You came when I called you.'

Thanking children is also a way of getting the message across that they are in control of their behaviour.

'Thanks for being on time.'

'You cleared up your toys, thank you.'

'Thanks for letting your brother have a go.'

Using lots of praise to improve behaviour does not come naturally. Louise was stuck in such a negative cycle with Josh that it took her ages to even notice when he was doing the right thing, let alone praise him for it. With practice, Louise began to use descriptive praise more frequently, and started to notice how it was improving Josh's behaviour.

When parents do praise, they should not make reference to things that have gone wrong in the past. Praise should not be qualified. 'You were really good today! Much better than yesterday when you were really naughty,' is a really unhelpful way of praising. It's like a friend saying, 'Those shoes are much nicer than that revolting pair you usually wear.'

Remember that praise for young children should always be backed up with lots of hugs and kisses.

Isn't It A Bit False?

Using the 6 to 1 ratio with children may sound contrived and even artificial at first. It is important that the praise is genuine, and there is no point in praising children for things they haven't done – you'll soon get rumbled. Some of Dean's teachers disliked him so much that they felt it would be hypocritical to say anything positive to him. I had to convince them that they didn't need to like him to notice that he had come into the class quietly and got his work out. Descriptive praise is always genuine because it focuses on what the child has just done. It doesn't have to be something amazing or spectacular – the parent is simply noticing and commenting on something the child has done right, because they want him to do it again.

Parents can be suspicious about giving out lots of praise. They think they will turn their children into spoilt brats with no self-motivation. Praising is especially hard for parents who were themselves brought up in a low-praise environment, since we tend to base our parenting style on our own upbringing. This is particularly true for parents under stress: when challenged by their children's behaviour, they tend to use their mother's or father's voice to regain control. Louise was comfortable telling Josh off as her mother kept reminding her that naughty children deserve to be reprimanded.

Think Potty-Training

Listen to the language parents use when they are potty-training their children. You will hear a constant barrage of praise for every little effort the child makes. This praise is often backed up with sticker charts and rewards. Parents know that if they tell children off and get angry every time there is an accident, the child will get turned off the whole process and things will only get worse. However annoying these accidents are, parents usually manage to stay resolutely positive. They have heard of Freud's musing on the subject and they are worried that unsuccessful potty-training could scar the child – and their carpets – for life.

When things go wrong during potty-training, parents increase the amount of praise and focus on small successes. They know there is no alternative to praising and that if they stick at it, they will get there in the end.

If you are prepared to try it, you will find that this simple model works for changing any sort of undesirable behaviour.

The Negative Cycle

Parents often get into a habit of constantly nagging their children. It's surprisingly easy to lose the habit of praising children when they behave well and only focus on the negatives. When children do what they are supposed to, nothing is said – the parents just think, 'Thank God it's quiet for a minute.' Josh realised that the only consistent way to get attention was by behaving badly: he would be noticed instantly and would always provoke a reaction. This started a pattern. Soon the currency of attention became overwhelmingly negative and Josh's behaviour became worse. It's depressing for parents like Louise, who feel they spend their whole time nagging; and it's depressing for the children, who are moaned at all the time.

Let's look at how the 6 to 1 strategy helped Mark and his three-year-old son Leo.

Mark and Leo's Day Out

Mark and his son Leo have been asked out to lunch with some friends who don't have children and have a house full of exciting, valuable and breakable ornaments displayed on tables just at Leo's height. Mark is nervous, because last time Leo broke a picture frame. As they arrive, Mark gives Leo a pep talk.

'Leo, we need to be really careful in this house. Last time you broke a nice picture and I was very sad. If you touch anything I tell you not to today, I will take you straight home and you won't be able to go to Granny's tomorrow.' Mark has tried to make a plan with Leo, but because he has started to go into reptile mode it's not a very good one. In effect, he has said to Leo, 'If you are bored or you want my attention, all you have to do is grab one of those tempting trinkets.' He then made a threat that he almost certainly won't be able to carry out. Mark has told Leo what he doesn't want him to do, but he hasn't told him what he should do instead.

Mark gives Leo one last reminder as they walk through the house. 'Remember, don't touch anything.' In other words, 'Remember how you can get my attention if you are bored.' He sets Leo up on the carpet with some toy animals and, as Leo starts to play happily, Mark begins to relax and enjoy his lunch and his glass of wine. Fifteen minutes later, Mark is engrossed in a conversation with his host about house prices; Leo, meanwhile, has started to grow tired of the farm animals. A china dog on a table catches his eye and he goes to investigate. Mark doesn't notice until Leo has it in his hand.

'Put that down at once,' he shouts, leaping from his seat. He grabs the dog and puts it on a high shelf out of Leo's reach. Mark finds a book, puts Leo on his lap and reads him a story. When he has finished, Leo plays for a few more minutes and then goes over to look at a vase of flowers. He gets holds of a freesia and tries to pull it away from the bunch. The vase topples over and water spills all over Leo and the carpet. Mark is furious. He is also embarrassed, because he can feel the disapproval of his friends. He leads Leo out into the hall and hisses through clenched teeth:

'Will you stop fiddling with things! I told you not to in the car. If you do it again we are going home. Okay? Okay? Do you understand?'

Mark is trying to give maximum threats with minimum volume. Leo thinks this is funny and starts to laugh.

'Just watch it,' says Mark.

They go back to the lunch table and there is a little more peace. Leo has decided he would like some more attention, so he climbs on to the sofa and tries to reach the china dog. Mark pulls him down and in the process bangs Leo's head against a lamp. Leo screams his head off while Mark tries to put the lampshade back on. The friends look horrified and priggish; Mark feels like tipping his glass of wine over their heads. Mark picks up Leo and they leave.

Result: the visit was a disaster and Mark probably won't be asked back with Leo in tow.

How Could Mark Have Used the 6 to 1 Strategy?

To begin with, Mark's initial plan could have been made when he was feeling calmer and better able to think clearly. He should have prepared Leo for a successful visit by describing exactly how he wanted him to behave and offering a reward if he managed it.

'When we get to the house you will see lots of interesting things, but you have to be very careful with them and not touch anything unless Daddy is with you. If you see something you would like to look at, ask me and I will get it down and we can look at it together. Do you think you can do that?'

'Yes.'

Leo is now excited about going out and he knows how to get his father's attention if he wants it.

When they arrived, Mark could have explained his plan to his hosts. It's better to be upfront about what is going to happen, rather than react when the problems begin.

As soon as Leo started playing with the animals, Mark should have jumped in with some praise.

'You're playing with your animals, Leo, well done.'

He could then have given Leo some attention every few minutes with a few words of praise.

'Leo, you are playing so well with the animals.'

'Good playing, Leo.'

'Leo, you're being really careful.'

This praise gives Leo the attention he needs and reminds him how to get more attention. Mark doesn't need to be intrusive or spoil the flow of the playing – it's as if he's punctuating Leo's game. By giving out little packets of praise, it is likely that Leo will concentrate for longer and Mark will have a chance to chat to his friends. When Leo starts to get bored with the animals, Mark can offer to read him a story as a reward for playing so well. Instead of using the story as a bribe to stop Leo from grabbing ornaments, he is using it as a reward for doing the right thing.

'Leo, you played so well with the animals that I want to read you a story.'

If Leo starts to wander round the room, Mark can remind him what to do if he wants to touch something. Leo points at the dog and Mark can give him some more praise: 'You remembered to tell me if you wanted to look at something.'

Mark can then get the dog down and can supervise Leo

while he looks at it. If it's really fragile, Mark keeps hold of it; if not, he can show Leo how to handle it carefully.

'Leo, you're holding the dog really carefully.'

'You put the dog down really gently.'

'You gave me the dog back when I asked you to.'

The opportunities to praise Leo are there all the time. Leo is getting lots of attention, but he's getting it on Mark's terms and he is learning valuable lessons: how to behave in someone else's house and how to look at precious things without smashing them.

If Leo does decide to grab at something valuable, then Mark should remove the object, get down to his level, gently hold his shoulders and look into his eyes without smiling and remind him not to touch. Seconds later, he can praise him for being careful. When it's time to go, Mark can give Leo lots of praise for behaving well. Mark may feel embarrassed giving so much praise out in front of his friends, especially if he isn't used to it. But he will be a lot less embarrassed than he would be if his son started trashing the place and they had to leave in a hurry.

How to Praise: A Summary

1 Praise should explicitly describe the good behaviour; this means the child will know what to do to get praised again.

2 Praise should be genuine.

3 Exaggerated, over-the-top praise should be avoided.

4 Praise should not contain veiled criticism or negative comparisons.

5 Using lots of descriptive praise will not turn your children into spoilt brats.

tools for supporting better behaviour

6

rewards

This chapter shows how the appropriate use of small rewards can help to improve children's behaviour. It will help parents to avoid the pitfalls of over-rewarding, being inconsistent and ending up with children who become dependent on being rewarded. If used in conjunction with the 6 to 1 strategy, simple rewards will help to change the most difficult behaviours.

Why Should I Reward My Child for Doing What He Should be Doing Anyway?

I am surprised by how many parents and teachers ask this question, getting hot under the collar at the idea of rewarding a child's good behaviour. The answer is: because it works.

We are motivated by two types of reward – *intrinsic*, the pride you feel when you achieve something such as learning to ride a bicycle, and *extrinsic*, a physical reward you receive for doing something, such as getting a sweet from your mother when you learn to ride a bicycle. We bring children into a world in which extrinsic rewards for success are openly displayed, from Porsches to gold earrings. We are motivated by other people noticing our achievements and successes. Children are no different.

How do you feel if nobody at work notices what a good job you are doing? If your boss put a star chart up in the boardroom and gave out certificates at the end of the week for the best employee, you would think it was infantile nonsense. However, despite yourself, you'd still get a little buzz when you got a star and you'd certainly notice who won the certificate each week. We have an in-built need to be noticed and we like this need to be backed up with something tangible.

Imagine your boss deciding that despite all the hard work you have put in over the year, there will be no Christmas bonuses. After all, why do you need additional money for what you should be doing anyway? We can hardly be surprised that children are similarly motivated, and as parents we can use this to our advantage.

We would love children to need only intrinsic rewards, to get dressed in the morning purely for that sense of pride that comes with a job well done. The problem is that children do not have the foresight that adults have. Children can't see that if they get dressed quickly, then they can be at school on time, so they are ready to learn, so they will pass their exams, so they will get into university, so they will get a good job, so they will be happy, successful and rich ... Adults have this foresight and yet even we find it hard to do what we ought to do. We all know that if we take more exercise and don't eat so much we are going to be healthier. Yet how many times did you go to the gym last month? Did you resist that chocolate biscuit? There is a constant tension within us between what we should do, what we want to do and what we can be bothered to do.

Children may have really good reasons why they don't do what they are supposed to do. If they are enjoying playing with their toys, why should they want to stop to do something as boring, difficult and frustrating as getting dressed? And it may well be that they get more parental attention if they don't get dressed – if they really stall, their mother could become so fed up that she might get them dressed herself.

As we saw in the previous chapter, the good news is that the most effective reward of all for a child is free and easily to hand – praise. Simply noticing children doing the right thing will make them more likely to do it again. Sometimes, however, children slip into a pattern of behaviour that has become embedded and praise alone is not enough to do the job. The child may have begun to get some sort of pay-off for the behaviour, however negative it may seem, and it can become necessary to use rewards to help to change things.

A well-thought-out and consistent system of rewards, with lots of descriptive praise built in, will change the most ingrained, challenging patterns of behaviour.

Rewards given for general good behaviour are not as effective as rewards for specific targets. The reward needs to be agreed in advance with the child and it should be easy to administer. If the child meets the target then he has to receive the reward irrespective of what else has been going on. Rewards should not be expensive or hugely time-consuming. It is not the size of the reward, but the inevitability that will change the behaviour. They are also a lot more fun to dish out than punishments.

In this chapter we will look at some easy-to-use reward systems like pebbles in the jar and target sheets that will help to change children's behaviour.

Emily and the Eggs

I recently worked with Clare and her six-year-old daughter Emily. In Emily's first year at school, Clare had successfully sold her the idea that now she was at big school she needed to dress herself. Emily was proud of getting dressed on her own and being all ready to leave for school at 8.15am. Recently, however, things had started to slip. Emily had begun to dawdle and they were getting later and later. Clare was having to make Emily's packed lunch and then rush up and chivvy Emily into her clothes. It had now reached the stage where Clare had begun to dress Emily and clean her teeth for her. Clare was increasingly bad-tempered in the morning and the walk to school, which had always been a special time for them, was becoming a sulky trudge. Clare felt angry and guilty in equal measure and Emily just moaned.

Clare checked with the school, but Emily was apparently very happy there. Clare decided to use a sticker chart to motivate Emily. If she got dressed on her own she received a sticker. If she managed it five days running, Clare would take her to the cinema at the weekend. The first week, this worked like a charm. Clare had made a bright chart and had bought a book of stickers. She explained her plan to Emily who was delighted by the challenge. Emily appeared suited and booted in the kitchen at eight o'clock every day that week and Clare made a big song and dance about letting her put her sticker on the chart.

On Friday, Emily talked all the way to school about the film they were going to go and see. Clare was a bit quieter, for she had looked in her diary and realised that on Saturday Emily had a birthday party that was going to take up most of the day and on Sunday they were booked in for lunch with the in-laws.

'Darling, I'm really sorry, but I think we're going to have to put off the cinema until next weekend. We're just too busy. You don't want to miss Daisy's party tomorrow and on Sunday we are going to Granny's. We'll definitely go next weekend, I promise.'

Emily was a bit deflated, but Clare was relieved that she seemed to take the disappointment pretty well.

The following Monday, Emily got dressed on her own again. Clare was so delighted and relieved that she gave her two stickers. She also gave her one in the evening for eating her tea without a fuss. On Tuesday, Emily threw a bit of a strop when she only got one sticker for getting dressed so Emily said she could have another one if she walked to school nicely. Emily negotiated three more stickers for various good works around the house. By Friday, Clare had run out of stickers, so instead she wrote a couple of IOUs on Post-it notes that she stuck on the chart. At the weekend, Emily didn't want to see any of the films that were on at the local cinema and Clare didn't have time to go further afield.

The next week, Emily stopped getting dressed on her own. Clare offered her three sticker IOUs but the motivation seemed to have gone and Clare resorted to dressing Emily, while nagging her for being such a baby.

When I went to visit, Clare and I talked about the sticker chart. She was still using it from time to time and she produced it from behind a load of papers on a pinboard. It was looking dog-eared and tired and it was covered with a combination of stickers, Post-its and scribbled notes saying 'well done' for this and that.

I wanted to help Clare resurrect a reward system but I felt the sticker chart had run its course. I spotted a wooden bowl holding some beautiful marble eggs. I suggested we base our rewards on them as they were big, attractive and heavy. Clare talked through the target again with Emily – 'Dress myself and be down to breakfast by eight o'clock' – and asked her to suggest a reward that she would like. Clare was surprised by what Emily chose if she earned five eggs in a week: 15 minutes of special playtime with her mother on Saturday.

Before I left, I explained the five golden rules for rewards to Clare. I particularly emphasised that she mustn't devalue the eggs by giving them out for anything except getting dressed. Nor should she let

Emily have more than one at a time. I also made certain that Clare understood the importance of granting Emily her fifteen minutes of special play and that it needed to be exactly fifteen minutes, no less and no more, however much fun they were having. This was important, because if one week Clare spent twenty-five minutes playing and the next week she could only spare thirteen, then the whole process would have been undermined and devalued. Consistency is the key.

We spoke on the phone four weeks later and Clare said there had been a huge improvement. Emily had earned her reward again and again and they had both really enjoyed the special playtime. Clare wanted to start using the eggs in the bowl for bedtimes, but I suggested they work on mornings for one more week to embed the new behaviour and then to give the whole thing a rest for at least a month. With any reward, the excitement and pantomime goes after a bit and the motivation from both parent and child wanes. The other unexpected outcome was that Clare rediscovered the fun of playing with Emily. Previously, their lives had become a rush from school to playdate, to party without any time to muck about together.

Making Rewards Work: The Five Golden Rules

1. *Use the reward to change one specific behaviour*
Parents often use sticker charts or reward systems as a way of recognising generally good behaviour. This

is not effective as it is too unfocused. The child doesn't really know what to do to earn the rewards: sometimes they get them and sometimes they don't. With this system the parent's mood is often the main factor in deciding whether a reward has been earned or not. If you have lost your temper earlier in the evening, you will give out lots of rewards later on to assuage your guilt. You will give out more rewards on a Friday because the weekend is coming and your tolerance levels are higher. These fairly random rewards also encourage children to start trying to make deals:

'Come on, Mum, I ate all my food, can I have a reward?' Or, 'Mum, if I eat all my food can I have a reward?'

When using rewards, focus on one bit of behaviour you want to change. Don't be tempted to go for the most complicated or annoying, but choose something that would make everyone's life better if it went away. Tell the child specifically what you do want to see them doing, not what you don't want to see. Only give the reward for this behaviour, give it every time you see it and never give out the reward for anything else.

2. *Keep the reward small*
Parents often feel that they need to have a spectacular reward to motivate their children. This is not the case. As we saw in the case study, Emily chose a surprisingly small but, to her, important reward.

Also remember that what motivates the child is often not the reward itself but the certainty that if they meet their target, they *will* get it. This is particularly the case with children under eight. They like the pantomime and excitement of achieving and the recognition and praise they get from their parents. Like Christmas, it's the anticipation of the stocking that excites them, rather than what is actually inside.

If you've decided to let your child chose her own reward but she is finding this hard, offer her a range of little things she can choose from.

3. *Make sure you deliver*

If your child has earned a reward, make sure she gets it as soon as possible. The younger the child, the less time she can wait. She needs to associate the reward with the new behaviour, so once she has earned the agreed amount of stickers, marbles or eggs, don't put it off. If the link between the behaviour and reward goes, the behaviour won't change. When you devise a reward, be certain to check that you really can deliver. It's not the size of the consequence, but its inevitability that will change the behaviour.

4. *Have a time limit*

If you focus on changing one particular piece of behaviour as suggested, this method shouldn't take more than a month. If you haven't seen a substantial change in that time, your target is almost certainly too difficult for the child and you will need to think again.

The first week should see the child enthusiastic about winning the reward and it will often go very well. During the second week, the child will at times try out the old behaviour to see how serious you are about change and – subconsciously – to compare which behaviour gets the better emotional pay-off. During the third week things will start to really change and the fourth week gives a chance for the behaviour to become embedded. Once this has happened, you and the child can formally end the reward and target. Parents often keep the reward system going for ages, because they think that if they stop it then the child will go back to the old behaviour. This is rarely the case. Once the pattern has been broken, it doesn't usually restart. Children will associate the formal ending of the reward system with a positive outcome and will move on from it. Children don't want to be in trouble all the time, they can just get stuck for a bit in a negative pattern. If you let a reward system go on too long it loses its impact, the parent tires of the panto and the child loses interest in the reward.

After one successful campaign against a particular bit of bad behaviour, it is tempting to go straight into another. Resist. Take a good few weeks out before you decide to have another go. If the reward doesn't feel fresh and exciting then it won't work nearly as well.

Successful reward systems also have a positive effect on parents. They help them to focus on what is going well, rather than on the negatives, and they quite naturally increase the praise to criticism ratio nearer to 6 to 1.

5. *Don't mess with rewards*

Never take away rewards from children as a punishment. Rewards are earned and once earned need to be delivered. This is why they work best when they are focused on specific behaviour – when you see that behaviour, the child earns the reward. If your child is being really difficult just when you are due to give him a reward, it's fine to postpone it for a short amount of time. Don't be afraid to explain your decision. After all, you need to be in the right frame of mind. You can say something like, 'You will get the reward in ten minutes when you are calm.' Or, 'I am too cross to give you the reward now, we will have it in half an hour.'

Don't have one of those 'Right!' moments and tell your child you are cancelling the reward. If you do, all the hard work that you have both put in will be lost.

Rewards: Some Pitfalls

Over-Rewarding

Don't fall into the pitfall of over-rewarding. If your child is expecting to get one sticker for getting dressed, then it must be only one sticker. If you give out two because you are in a good mood and your child is being especially sweet then you devalue the process.

Siblings

Trying to change a bit of behaviour of one of your children can often cause jealousy and resentment from their siblings. If you are running a reward system with a younger child, you can explain the process to older children and engage their help. 'We are trying to help your brother get dressed in the morning, so he doesn't make us late for school. Do you think you could encourage him as well? He often listens to you more than to me.'

If the children are close in age and jealousy over attention and praise is an issue, then there are two possible solutions. You can make it into a team effort, so the two of them work together. 'Every time you both get dressed in the morning you can have a sticker. If you have earned five by the end of the week, you can have a telly breakfast on Saturday morning together.' The child you are not targeting, because he is good at getting dressed, will be able to encourage the slowcoach. They have to work as a team which encourages sibling harmony and teamwork.

The alternative is to set a target for the sibling to work on as well. It may be that there isn't something obvious, but if you ask the child he will usually think of something. The children can earn their own rewards without needing to be jealous. Keep the focus positive. 'Well done, you earned another sticker,' and avoid negative comparisons such as, 'Your brother got a sticker today but you're not going to.'

Unachievable Rewards

I once did some work with a mother who had set up a reward system for her difficult son. Their relationship had become very negative and she found herself constantly shouting at him. The boy, Daniel, was incredibly challenging and refused to do what he was asked much of the time and threw spectacular tantrums. He was very clever a making at scene when his mother was most likely to give in, for example when they were out in public, or round at friends' houses. We talked about the range of behaviours he was showing and how the reward chart fitted in.

'When he is good for a whole week, he gets to go to the shop and I buy him a treat costing ten pounds. We've been doing it for a year,' Daniel's mother told me.

'That sounds great,' I said. 'How many ten-pound trips has he had?'

'None!' she replied. 'Can you believe it? He hasn't had one good week in a whole year!'

She had missed the point of rewarding behaviour completely. It is essential that the reward is attainable and the child achieves it regularly. An unachievable reward has no motivational power and does nothing for the child's self-esteem. The reward is dangled over him as a constant reminder of his failure.

Unreasonable Expectations

Take into account the age and maturity of your child when you set a reward target. Just because an older sibling could meet the target when he was a similar age does not mean all your children will be able to. If you set a reward system up and the child is not earning rewards, then you have set the bar too high and you are expecting too much. Choose something they definitely can achieve if they put in some effort.

Think of it like reading: we wouldn't expect our child to embark on *War and Peace* once they have learnt their initial letter sounds – and we shouldn't have unreasonable expectations of their behaviour either.

Which Rewards Work?

The best rewards are those that are easy to deliver, small and chosen by the child.

It is really effective for children to be working towards a reward, but have each success marked by a token.

Pebbles in the Jar

Pebbles in the jar is a highly effective reward system. It is easy to set up, adaptable and children love it. Parents I have worked with have been able to use pebbles in the jar to change all kinds of challenging behaviour.

You will need:

- One old jam jar
- A handful of pebbles from the garden, washed

The pebbles in the jar are used to help change a habit of irritating everyday behavioural patterns that have not been changed by the 6 to 1 strategy. The theory is simple:

■ *Planning*

Make a plan when you are relaxed and calm, decide the behaviour you want to get rid of and remember to work out what you want to see instead. It is essential that the pebbles in the jar method is only applied to changing one particular behavioural problem at a time.

■ *Setting it up*

Explain the behaviour you want to see to your child, tell them they will get a pebble every time you see the behaviour. Once they have got a certain amount of pebbles, they will get a reward.

■ *Choosing a reward*

It is important that the reward is small and manageable and it is essential that if the child has earned the pebbles, he gets the reward. If the parent is unable to give the reward for any reason then the whole exercise becomes a waste of time. Remember, it is not the size of the consequence, but the inevitability that will change behaviour.

■ *Do a rehearsal*

Demonstrate the behaviour you want to see and then get the child to have a go. When they do it give out lots of praise, make the process seem exciting. Then let the child pick up a pebble and put it in the jar. There is something about the ritual of this that children love.

■ *Put it into action*

Whenever the child follows his target, let him get a pebble and put it in the jar. Always do this instantly. When he has got the amount you agreed on, give him the reward.

■ *Finishing*

When the child has earned his reward a few times and the behaviour has become habit, stop the process. Parents always worry that this will be very difficult, and that the child will start to behave as before in order to get the reward again. In my experience, once the new behaviour is embedded, children gain an intrinsic reward from it and continue without the reward scheme.

Do not start trying to change another bit of behaviour as soon as the pebbles in the jar target has been met. Give the child a breather of a few weeks in order to consolidate the behaviour. If you need to change more behaviour, relaunch pebbles in the jar but think of a different, exciting, but easy-to-administer reward.

I used pebbles in the jar to help my own children to share their room better at night. Bedtimes had become difficult and the children carried on talking and singing far too late, even though they were exhausted. It meant they were not getting enough sleep and were grumpy in the mornings.

To earn a pebble they had to stay in bed and stop talking when my wife or I told them it was time to go to sleep.

They each had their own jar and for every pebble they got during the week they could have a Smartie with their breakfast – not healthy, I admit, but because my daughter was only two she needed instant gratification to keep her on target. If they managed five pebbles in a week they got twenty minutes of television time on a Saturday morning.

Some days one or both didn't get a pebble and there were tears and tantrums. They needed to test whether we were serious. When they realised that we were going to stick to the deal, they began to go to sleep on time. Now, touch wood, they share very well.

Pebbles in the Jar in Action: Mark, Four and Daniel, Six

The pebbles in the jar method is particularly useful for sorting out a problem between two children. A mother recently asked me to help her with her sons, aged four and six, who were constantly squabbling and seemed unable to share their toys. The mother had got into the habit of yelling at the boys whenever they fought, and fighting had become a way of getting guaranteed attention. We set up a pebbles in the jar system to help the boys to share. We explained what we wanted to see and the language we wanted to hear. Then we got the boys to rehearse.

Whenever the boys played well the mother told them she had noticed and got them to put a pebble in the jar. It helped her to be more positive and escape her cycle of nagging. The boys realised that by co-operating they could fill the jar more quickly and because they were working together for a common goal they began to support and encourage each other.

When the jar was full they were allowed to eat a mango or an orange in the bath, an easy-to-administer reward that they loved. It took three weeks for the new behaviour to become embedded and, when it did, the boys stuck with it because they had lost the habit of arguing and now enjoyed playing together.

The Target Sheet

You will need:

- A large piece of paper
- A photo, or picture, of your child behaving well
- One packet of stickers

The target sheet is effective for changing more serious behaviour. Often parents can be dealing with a whole range of challenges, but it is important to begin with just one piece of behaviour they want to change.

First, take a photograph or do a drawing of your child rehearsing the new behaviour you want to see. Work with your child to decide on how many stickers he needs to earn a reward. The picture is put on to the target sheet as a reminder for the child and they get a sticker whenever they manage the new pattern of behaviour. The target sheet is displayed prominently so your child can be reminded of the target. At the end of the week, if he has received enough stickers, he gets the reward. With older children there can be a menu of rewards that they can work towards. Children can choose to bank a week's stickers and save up for a bigger reward.

You can use target sheets for two or more children. For example, take a photograph of all of your children, standing in the hall, ready to go to school on time. When they all manage to do this give them a sticker, when they have got five stickers, they get a communal reward such as a film night with popcorn.

Target Sheet for Jamie

Jamie was out of control when I first met him. His mother Sarah had recently had a new baby and she was exhausted. Jamie was not getting the attention he had been used to before the birth and he had worked out that the best way to get his mother to notice him was to hurt the baby. Mother and son had got into such a spiral that she felt she was shouting at him almost all the time. On one occasion she had screamed, 'I hate you.'

We set up a target sheet for Jamie that had a photo of him stroking the baby's tummy. His target was to be gentle. Sarah showed him all the things he could do to earn a sticker such as singing the baby a song, playing peek-a-boo and reading stories. His reward if he managed to get twenty stickers in a week was to spend some special time with his mother away from the rest of the family.

Jamie now realised he had a role with the baby and so he felt more included and less ignored. The target sheet helped Sarah to get back into the habit of paying him positive attention. The change in Jamie was quite dramatic: in two days he had stopped hurting the baby and within three weeks his attention-seeking had significantly reduced.

Rewards: A Summary

1 We are all motivated by rewards.

2 Children can't see the long-term effects of behaving well and rewards help them to get back on track in the short-term. Change won't always be instant and parents will need to keep going even when they don't seem to be getting anywhere.

3 Rewards should be used to change a specific piece of behaviour. Only reward that behaviour, don't give out rewards for other things, however good the child is being. You will confuse the child and water down the impact of the reward.

4 Rewards should be small, cheap and easy to administer. Don't be afraid to give out lots at first, the child has to see quickly what is in it for him.

5 It is not the size of the reward but the certainty of receiving it that will change behaviour.

6 Children should receive rewards as soon as possible after the good behaviour – the younger the child, the shorter the delay.

7 Use pebbles in the jar or target sheets so children learn to work towards a reward.

8 Don't keep reward systems going for too long. They will start to lose their impact.

9 Don't have unreasonable expectations of your children. The target must be achievable or the child will never get the reward.

10 Never, ever, ever, take rewards away. If the child has earned the reward, by achieving the target you agreed, he must get it. You can delay the delivery if he is being a real pain, but he must get it sooner rather than later.

punishment, consequences and time out

In this chapter I will demonstrate how parents can use punishment or consequences in a positive way to change behaviour. I will suggest suitable consequences for bad behaviour and show how having a calm, positive approach will help the child to learn from their mistakes and make them less likely to make the same ones again. I will show how to use time out as an effective sanction for poor behaviour as part of a plan to bring about change.

I was once talking to a headteacher of a school in south London who had a number of difficult pupils. 'What we need,' she said, 'is a punishment for these boys which really works, something that will stop them ever daring to misbehave again.'

'We could shoot them,' I wanted to say, 'you wouldn't get much trouble from them then.' She had fallen into the same trap as many parents: if the punishment is harsh enough, then the bad behaviour will go. The problem is that punishment, on its own, is not enough to improve behaviour. Punishing children can make adults feel powerful and in control. It gives them the sense that they are actually doing something about bad behaviour, but it is more often a way for them to show their anger and frustration, rather than part of a process that changes behaviour.

When I give talks for parents or teachers and I get on to the subject of punishment I always see some people in the audience sit up and begin to take notice. 'We've got through all that fluffy stuff about rewards and praise,' they seem to be thinking, 'now we can get on to the real thing. What these children need is proper discipline. I had it when I was a child and it never did me any ...'

What people often seem to forget is that it was always the same boys getting caned in those dark days. If a good thrashing was so effective at controlling behaviour, you would think you wouldn't need to use it more than once. There is surely something wrong with a system of discipline that relies on fear and punishment to get children to conform.

I believe strongly that parents should be strict about keeping to rules, but children should be able to learn to test the boundaries, take some risks and get things wrong without being made to suffer for it. Punishment is only effective in changing behaviour if it is balanced with a clear plan that includes lots of praise and rewards.

Consequences vs Punishments

Traditionally, the thinking went, if you were hard enough on children and had suitably harsh punishments, they would be cowed, by fear, into behaving. The difficulty is if the result of stepping out of line is too severe, then children will learn to operate only to please the adults around them and will be frightened of taking risks. Imagine how worried you would be if your child never did anything wrong! We should be wanting our children to test out boundaries and find out how far they can go.

It is more effective to think in terms of consequences than punishments when dealing with behaviour. The focus is on helping children to see what they have done wrong and, more importantly, helping them not to do it again. The notion of a consequence links the outcome to the behaviour and stops the punishment being arbitrary and irrelevant.

Using Consequences
John had been brought up in a very strict household in which fear of punishment had been the main incentive to behave. He was married to Kate who had a rather more liberal upbringing and when they came to see me this conflict of parenting styles was causing problems of consistency with their three-year-old son, Tommy. Tommy was in the habit of throwing his food on the floor if he didn't like it. Kate, who did most of the childcare, was in the habit of picking up the food and putting it in the bin. John felt it was time to get tough

with Tommy and decreed that whenever he threw his food on the floor he would be punished by being sent to his room and getting nothing more to eat. Kate thought this was much too strict and when John was not there she continued to let Tommy get away with throwing food. While talking to John and Kate, I convinced them that they would have to work together and that they would need to agree on a plan to change Tommy's behaviour. John wanted Kate to get tougher with Tommy; Kate wanted John to be less punitive. I persuaded Kate that there needed to be a consequence for throwing food on the floor, otherwise Tommy was going to keep on doing it. On the other hand, I felt that John's punishment was very harsh and didn't teach Tommy what he should be doing. We set up a system whereby Tommy would get a pebble when he got through a mealtime without throwing any food. When he got three pebbles he got to watch ten minutes extra television with his mother. In addition, if Tommy kept his food on the plate he would get a story straight away with his mother. If he threw his food on the floor he would have to clear it up before he could have his story. If he didn't clear it up then he didn't get the story.

For the first two days, Tommy was perfect, then he tried to push it. He wanted to see if Kate was really going to insist that he tidied up before he got his story. He threw his food on the floor and at the end of the meal demanded a story and a pebble. I had prepared Kate for this and told her she had to tough it out. The outcome was a tantrum of epic proportions. John came *in during the middle of it and was able to offer moral support to Kate. Tommy didn't clear up and he didn't get his story. The next day she was dreading breakfast, again Tommy threw his food on the floor, but Kate calmly asked him to tidy up and then sat on the sofa holding his favourite book. After a bit of stomping around Tommy did a reasonable job of clearing up (for a three-year-old) and he got his story. This carried on for a couple more days and then Tommy stopped throwing food.*

John and Kate were able to change Tommy's behaviour by making a clear link between the behaviour and the consequence. He realised tidying up is boring, having stories is more fun and behaving well earns pebbles, which in turn earn some time in front of the television with Mum.

Consequences need to guide children away from doing the wrong thing and stop them getting into damaging patterns of behaviour, without squashing their spirit.

As a teacher, I have come across children, often girls, who only seem to operate with the approval of the teacher. Everything they do or don't do is linked to this approval and they are constantly checking with the adult to make sure they are doing the right thing. I worry what happens to these children with an almost slavish focus on pleasing others. They may grow out of it, but I can't help feeling they are missing out on learning to be creative risk-takers.

So Where Do Consequences Fit in with Improving Behaviour?

First of all, it is important to remember that, on their own, consequences won't work. You will never be able to punish bad behaviour away. Like rewards, consequences need to be manageable. It is pointless having a consequence that is too difficult or complicated to impose.

Consequences should come as soon as possible after the crime. The younger the child, the more immediate the consequence needs to be. A consequence delayed for a day or two, or even an hour or two in the case of a three-year-old, will have no effect.

The aim of consequences is to get the child to stop whatever he is doing wrong, to learn from his mistake and be less likely to repeat it. Always try and give the child a choice before you impose the consequence – this means he is taking responsibility. 'If you keep annoying your sister, then you will lose ten minutes of television time,' is much more effective than, 'Right, that's it, you've lost ten minutes of television time.' When the behaviour is severe, however, then there doesn't need to be a warning and the consequence should be imposed straight away. If you do give out a consequence make sure you stick to it. Empty threats just say, 'Don't take me seriously.'

Withdrawal of Privileges
This can include anything from banning television or computer games for anything from a few minutes to a whole day. You can also withdraw some of your time,

such as limiting the amount of bedtime stories you will read. Taking away a favoured toy can be effective, as long as it is time-limited and the child knows what he has to do to get it back. With older children, you can try stopping playdates or not letting them go to an activity. With these sorts of consequences, you must have thought it through beforehand, otherwise you will have a reptile moment and you will come out with something too draconian. Give the child a warning in advance (if appropriate), and let him know what will happen if he continues being difficult. This gives him a chance to stop and will help you to stay out of reptile mode. When you are withdrawing privileges, only do it for a short period of time.

Logical Consequences: Making the Punishment Fit the Crime

The most useful consequences are those that follow logically from the crime so that children have to sort out whatever mess they have made. If they spill their food on the floor, they have to clear it up; if they don't do their homework, then next time they have to do it before they have tea or watch television. It becomes possible to educate the child so that he is deciding what the consequence should be. Children are usually surprisingly honest and quite hard on themselves. The point of these consequences is for the children to see the harm they have done and take responsibility for sorting it out.

Tips for Using Consequences

1. *Beware pay-offs*

I once worked with a family who had a very attention-seeking middle daughter, Bella. When she was being annoying, she was put in her room for five minutes. This was all very well, but then when she came out her mother would sit down and they would have a protracted heart-to-heart about her behaviour. This debrief lasted longer than the time out. The pay-off was obvious. For an attention-seeking child, a few minutes spent alone in her room was easily worth the ten minutes of her mother's undivided attention.

2. *Keep them small*

Bigger, more dramatic punishments won't change behaviour. The inevitability of the consequence will. If a child does something wrong, then the consequence must happen. If you are haphazard or erratic, then the message is that the bad behaviour matters more on some days than on others, such as when I am in a bad mood or when I have the energy to make a fuss.

I have worked with parents who have taken away a child's computer game for six weeks or have grounded children for a month. This can make the parent feel strict and in control, but in reality, the punishment is so harsh that the child feels he has blown it and there is no motivation for behaving.

This also fills the child with resentment and means the parent has nowhere to go if the behaviour doesn't improve.

3. *Use sparingly*

If you need to punish your children the whole time then something is not right. How much praise and positive attention are you giving out? Have you considered using rewards? Do you need to spend some time teaching your children how you want them to behave? Are your expectations too high?

Time Out

Time out is one of the most effective consequences for changing behaviour, but it needs to be used in the right way. It should be seen as a time when the child is away from the family for a short period of time during which he will get no attention. In effect, it is the withdrawal of the opportunity to receive praise.

Where Should Time Out Happen?

Time out should take place somewhere quiet and away from the main hub of the family, where the child cannot disturb anyone else and won't be disturbed. I send my children to their bedroom if they need time out, as it gets them away from everyone else and I find it easier to manage than a naughty step. Parents worry that if children have time out in their bedrooms, they will start playing with their toys and so it will lose its effect. In my experience, children don't do this, for by the time they have thought about getting their toys out and started playing, the time out is over. If your child does seem to be enjoying time out in his bedroom then use another space. It doesn't matter where, as long as it is out of the way of the rest of the family. You can use another room in the house, your own bedroom, the bottom of the stairs or a little chair in a corridor. If you are not too self-conscious, you can use time out anywhere, pointing to a spot on the ground and saying, 'Three minutes of time out!' I once worked with a brilliant nursery teacher who would give her very challenging pupils time out on school trips. She would take a timer with her and if children were out of line they would have to sit down and do their minutes. She once had a little boy sitting in the aisle doing three minutes of time out on a class trip to Tesco.

My feeling is that, as long as time out is used infrequently and positively, it really doesn't matter too much where it takes place. The most important thing is that when a parent imposes time out it can be followed through successfully without any distractions.

How Old Do Children Need to be for Time Out to Work?

Usually, at around two and a half to three, children began to have some understanding of their behaviour and can therefore make sense of a consequence. At this age, I would be very sparing with the use of time out, using it only for violent or very persistent behaviour and after a firm warning. I would be careful to be sure the child understands what's going on. Time out can be effective until children are ten or eleven.

How Long Should Children Spend in Time Out?

As short a time as possible. The advice is often a minute for each year of their life but I think that this is probably more than is necessary. For under-fives, two or three minutes is enough. Young children have no real concept of time and there's no point in leaving them in time out for ages. There is a danger that a child will become so resentful about being left in time out that he forgets why he was sent there in the first place and enraged by being ignored for so long. For older children, I would use five minutes as an absolute maximum. Remember, it is not the severity of the consequence, but its inevitability that will change the behaviour.

When Should I Use Time Out?

Time out is best used to change specific behaviour such as violence towards siblings, rudeness or deliberate damage. This should be part of a plan worked out in advance and shared with the child. It should, of course be backed up by rewards when the child does the right thing. It is essential with time out that the child understands what the alternative is to the behaviour, so be explicit about what is desirable. Remember, the cause will often be attention-seeking, so try to have a reward that involves some positive attention and make sure there is lots of praise when the child is being good. It is important that time out is used sparingly, otherwise it will soon lose its impact. If you are using time out more than two or three times a week it is probably too much. Time out should be your last resort, not the first port of call when dealing with bad behaviour.

Egg Timers

Young children don't have any idea about time. It is worth buying an egg timer to help them to understand time out. Focusing on the sand as it goes through the timer helps to calm them down and it will also stop you from forgetting about them and leaving them in time out for longer than you had intended: 'Wow, it's really quiet round here, I wonder why?!'

One-minute timers can be bought from children's or school catalogues; the bigger ones are best and they are fairly cheap. Older children can turn the minute-timer over themselves if they have got more than one minute of time out. With younger children, you can be in charge of the timer and keep it where they can see it, but out of their reach. Don't end time out early if your child is being really sweet and apologetic, or if he is crying his eyes out. If you do, you will teach him how to be sneaky and manipulative. Stick to the time you agreed – no more, no less.

Rehearsals

Don't use time out for the first time when your reptile brain is engaged and you are having a 'Right!' moment. If you are going to use it, make sure you have worked out when and how in advance. Before you start using time out, rehearse it with the child. You explain that from now on if he behaves in a certain way, he will be sent to time out. You then show him where he will have to sit and explain for how long. Ask him to imagine a scenario when he has done something wrong, then tell him to go to time out and practise walking there, sitting down and, if you are using one, getting the timer out. Rehearsals always feel a bit weird and artificial, but we use them a lot at my school and once you have got over the strangeness, you will find them really effective. Rehearsals are essential for young children who simply won't know what they are supposed to do, or why.

Running Away from Time Out

The first few times a child is put into time out, he will almost certainly be furious and may not be in the mood to accept it. He may run off, to find out if you are really serious. Sometimes children will try and turn this into a game. Rehearsing will help, because it will show the child that time out is limited, manageable and won't go on for ever.

If you child runs away from time out, calmly pick him up, without any eye contact, and sit him back down. You can also repeat, parrot-like, 'When you have done your three minutes you can come out.' Don't, however, get into any sort of debate about it or say things like, 'Come on, it won't take long' or, 'I will come and do it with you,' or, 'Okay, why don't you just do one minute today?' Time out is the withdrawal of the opportunity to receive attention, so make sure the child is not getting any. The first few times you send your child to time out, it may be really hard, but if you handle it right he will learn to do it. At my school, even the most troubled and difficult children accept being given time out after a while. As long as you back yourself and stick with it, you will succeed!

When bigger children run out of time out, picking them up becomes harder. Have a prepared consequence that you can use to threaten them with in the form of a choice. 'If you don't go to time out, then you won't be able to watch television tonight. It's up to you.' Whatever consequence you choose, make sure you can follow through with it and be certain it will carry some clout with them. When you initially rehearse time out, you can discuss the sanction they will get if they don't stay put. When they are calm they will see that it's much better to accept three minutes in time out than to blow something bigger that they really enjoy. The last thing you want is a situation when your child runs out of time out, you lose your temper, go into reptile mode, shout 'Right!' at the top of your voice and then come out with a ludicrous punishment that you will never be able to follow through.

After Time Out

When your child has finished their minutes in time out you want to have a moment of repair and reconciliation. This should be brief as you don't want the child to get so much out of kissing and making up that it makes the time out seem worth it. Go to where the child has finished and congratulate him for doing it so well. Then ask him why he was sent there in the first place. If he pretends he doesn't know, suggest he has a couple more minutes to think about it. This usually jogs his memory pretty quickly. You will have to use your judgement if you think he really can't remember, and remind him what happened. If he was unkind or hit someone else, ask him how that person might be feeling and ask how he could make them feel better. Then ask how he could handle it better next time. Give him a hug and tell him you love him, let him apologise if necessary and then he can rejoin the family with no hard feelings. The time out has happened, atonement has been achieved and the matter is left in the past. This part of the process should take no more than a minute or two at the most.

Time Out for Lucy

Natalie was having trouble with her five-year-old middle daughter Lucy, who was hitting both her older brother and her little sister. Whenever Lucy hit one of her siblings, Natalie shouted at her and told her to go to time out at the bottom of the stairs. Lucy would refuse to stay in time out and would come running back into the kitchen. Natalie would send her back, but in seconds she would be out again. Time out had become an attention-seeking game and Natalie would usually give up after two or three tries. Natalie was fed up with time out and was on the verge of abandoning it when I arrived to work with the family.

The first thing I did was to get Natalie to introduce a reward system so that Lucy would get positive attention when she was gentle with her siblings. We settled on pebbles in the jar, so whenever Lucy was being kind and playing nicely with her brother and sister she would get a pebble. The jar was big and I encouraged Natalie to be generous and not worry if she was putting ten or fifteen pebbles in a day. When the jar was full, Lucy was to get some special time with her mother. I then asked Natalie to talk to Lucy about what would happen if she did hurt one of her siblings. We explained time out and asked Lucy to practise it a few times. Lucy quite enjoyed the attention and praise she got doing these rehearsals. I had a feeling that Natalie was going to back down under the weight of one of Lucy's spectacular tantrums, so I asked her to call me every night for the first week, for a bit of moral support. It can really help having a buddy who you can talk to when you are making a stand like Natalie, especially if you are a single parent or your spouse is always at work. Inevitably, things are going to get a bit hairy for a few days. The child is likely to go back to the old way of doing things and will try to get you to react the way you used to.

When I spoke to Natalie the first evening, the rewards were working really well and she hadn't needed to send Lucy to time out. But the next evening, she called in tears. Lucy had hit little Candy and Natalie had sent her to time out. She had then spent the next hour in a battle with Lucy trying to get her to stay in her room for three minutes. As soon as Natalie had put Lucy in there, she would come *running out again. Natalie had followed through with our plan and had threatened that there would be no television for Lucy the following day. Lucy had said she didn't care and had run off. I reassured Natalie that she had done well and that the next day it was important that she followed through and didn't let Lucy watch television.*

Natalie called me again the next night, not feeling much better. She had stopped Lucy watching television, but it had caused an almighty row and in her ensuing rage Lucy had hit Candy again. Natalie had tried to send Lucy to time out, but again she had refused and came out of her room after a matter of seconds. Natalie had again used the threat about missing television and Lucy had pretended she didn't care. Natalie was all ready to give in, but I persuaded her to agree to keep going for the rest of the week.

The following day, she stopped Lucy from watching television again and this time Lucy had sulked round the place, but hadn't hit her sister. I reminded Natalie to keep giving out the rewards for being gentle and, if things were calm, to do another rehearsal for time out.

For a couple more days things were quiet and then Natalie called again. She had had a breakthrough. Lucy had hit her big brother, Natalie had sent her to time out and Lucy had done it. I congratulated Natalie and reminded her not to go too over the top in praising Lucy, as we didn't want her to be getting a pay-off from being sent to time out. The pebble jar was filled the next evening and Lucy got to have her special time. I encouraged Natalie to lay on the praise with a trowel so that Lucy associated all the attention with doing the right thing.

Over the next two months Lucy stopped hitting her siblings and her general behaviour improved. I recommended that Natalie should stop using pebbles in the jar, as any reward system usually runs out of steam after a time. I suggested that Natalie kept up the high levels of praise for Lucy and continued to make time for special moments when they could be together.

What was the main cause of this change in behaviour? I would argue it was the praise and rewards that made the most substantial difference, because rather than being the 'naughty one', Lucy was recast in a much more positive light to her mother, her siblings and, most importantly, to herself. The praise and rewards were backed up by the use of time out, giving Lucy clear and firm boundaries to her behaviour and also helping Natalie to feel in control.

Smacking

I don't smack my own children. I think being a teacher and programmed never to hit children has hard-wired me against it. My feeling is that with clear planning and lots of praise and rewards parents will avoid going into reptile mode and so will not smack their children. If you do lose it and end up smacking you child, don't get stuck in an introspective guilt trip about what a useless parent you are. Give the child a cuddle, tell him you love him and move on.

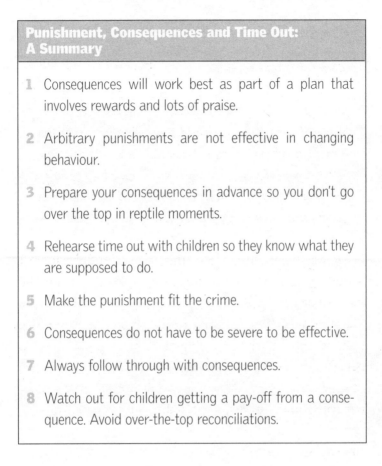

Punishment, Consequences and Time Out: A Summary

1 Consequences will work best as part of a plan that involves rewards and lots of praise.

2 Arbitrary punishments are not effective in changing behaviour.

3 Prepare your consequences in advance so you don't go over the top in reptile moments.

4 Rehearse time out with children so they know what they are supposed to do.

5 Make the punishment fit the crime.

6 Consequences do not have to be severe to be effective.

7 Always follow through with consequences.

8 Watch out for children getting a pay-off from a consequence. Avoid over-the-top reconciliations.

8

routines and rules

For many parents, it is the day-to-day routines of daily life that cause the most difficulty with children. During an average day, there are a whole load of things that the parent needs the child to do, that the child doesn't particularly like or want to do. Most are fairly mundane and uninteresting, such as getting dressed, cleaning teeth, tidying rooms and putting pyjamas on. Nevertheless they have to happen and by a certain time. This chapter will help parents to set up effective routines that get the boring bits out of the way, making room for less nagging and more fun. There is also a section here on using rules. When things are going wrong it is useful for parents to be explicit about what they want to see instead and have clear rules for the children to follow.

Routines

One of the most charming (and annoying) things about having a small child is that you are constantly asked to read the same story time and time again. When I get back from work and I am trying to have a cup of tea and a sit-down on the sofa, my two-year-old makes a beeline for me. Before I know what is happening he is sitting on my knee and shoving a book in my face.

'Read it, Daddy, read it, read it to me, Daddy.'

'I'm just having my tea, I'll read it in a minute.'

'But, Daddy, it's not fair! [Who taught him to say that?] Read it to me.'

He makes me feel guilty. I have a son who is actually interested in books. How can I be so cruel as to refuse?

'Okay, okay, we'll have the story.' He snuggles up against me.

I read the book with expression and do all the voices, putting everything into the performance. When I get to the end I put the book down, attempt to ease him off my lap and reach for my cold tea.

'But, Dad,' he says, 'read it again, please read it again, Dad please read the story.'

I relent, but when I finish five minutes later he won't let me rest. This time I do refuse and he bursts into tears and starts to badger my wife. One day, when I am feeling really patient, I might try and see how many times I would have to read the same story before he has had enough.

Why do two-year-olds enjoy this seemingly endless repetition? The answer is that it gives them a sense of security. Most of a two-year-old's life is organised by adults. They are told when to get up, what and when to eat, when to get dressed, who they see, where they go and when to go to bed. They have very little control over anything in their lives and they are often uncertain about what is going to happen next. When they find themselves in a new situation, they do not have the experience to be able to predict what is going to happen and how things are going to turn out. So the rereading of his favourite story gives my son a feeling of control. When the page turns, he knows what is going to happen next, he knows what each character is going to say and do and most importantly he knows how things are going to end. This feeling of control gives him a sense that he can influence the outcome of things to a satisfactory conclusion. It makes the world feel like a safer, more ordered place. From each rereading, my son will not only improve his language, he will also develop his understanding of other people's feelings and how they are likely to behave. This ability to predict what is likely to happen is a very important tool that children begin to develop when they start to reach the age of three.

This shows why, in an uncertain world, routines are so important to children. By knowing what is going to happen next, children feel safe and can develop a sense that things are going to turn out fine. What is, perhaps, surprising is that children with well-established routines cope better when things get chaotic and unpredictable than children whose lives are more disorganised. Many of the children I have worked with who have behaviour difficulties have terribly chaotic home lives. These children can find the smallest change hugely significant, because they cannot be confident that things are going to end up all right in the end. Children who do not have established routines feel less safe and often begin to develop their own rituals in order to help them gain a sense of control. These rituals can begin to take on a greater, disproportionate significance with anxious children and they can lead to signs of obsessive compulsive disorder (OCD). Children with OCD develop routines and rituals that begin to overtake their lives and can prevent them functioning at home and school in a normal way.

James's Bedtime Routine

I was recently called by a mother called Jenny who was having problems with her five-year-old son, James. Jenny's husband had got a new job, which meant he was spending significant periods of time away from home. James was missing his father enormously, had begun to play up constantly and his eczema had worsened. The situation wasn't helped by the fact that James's father usually did the disciplining. Jenny was so worried about James's unhappiness that she had begun to stretch many of the boundaries that had been established in the house. She often allowed James to stay up later to watch television, she was less insistent on making him eat his food and she had started helping him to brush his teeth and to dress in the morning. She wanted to go easy on James because he was so upset about his father and she felt he needed to be indulged. The problem was that when she gave him an inch he took a mile. When she tried to get him into bed he would throw a tantrum and scream and shout at her. He was refusing to eat anything that didn't contain significant amounts of sugar or saturated fat. Jenny swung between feeling sorry that James was so unhappy and furious that he was being such a brat. She was getting into rages with him because he was pushing her and then feeling horribly guilty afterwards. This guilt would lead to her being even more indulgent. When her husband did come back from his road trips he got fed up with having to come through the front door and re-establish discipline with James.

My advice was to tighten up on the routines in the house and to put aside her concerns about James feeling unhappy. We sat down when James was out on a playdate and planned routines for him. We agreed on a time for lights out (7.30pm) and then worked backwards from there. James would need to be in bed by 7.15pm so he could look at a book before the light went out. This meant he would need to be out of the bath by 6.30pm in order to have plenty of time to apply his eczema cream and put his pyjamas on and clean his teeth ready for a bedtime story at 6.45pm. There was to be no television after tea, which he would eat at the kitchen table at 5.30pm. When James came back, Jenny talked him through the routines so he would know exactly what was expected of him. We wrote out the routine and stuck a copy on the fridge door and in the bathroom so Jenny and James could refer to it when they needed to. It looked like this:

James's Bedtime Routine

5:00 Television or DVD
5:30 Tea
6:00 Upstairs for bath
6:30 Out of the bath, cream, pyjamas and teeth
6:45 Story time
7:15 In bed reading
7:30 Kiss goodnight and lights out

This was a more protracted bedtime than James had been used to, but I persuaded Jenny that, by stretching out the routine over a longer period, the two of them could go at a gentle pace and she would not constantly need to hurry him. It also gave James lots of time to talk about missing his father – and Jenny the chance to give James lots of love and reassurance. Jenny used pebbles in the jar to help James stick to the new plan. If he had followed his routine satisfactorily, then he was allowed to put a pebble in the jar before Jenny put the light out. When he got five pebbles, he was allowed to start watching television at 4.45pm. I encouraged Jenny to be really tight with the routine for the first three weeks until it was fully established. Much to her surprise, James really liked having a routine. He would check where they had got to on the list in the bathroom and kitchen and asked to have a copy in his room as well. Within a few days, he was prompting and reminding her when it was time for the next thing to happen. James continued to miss his father,

but there was a marked improvement in his behaviour.
When I saw them again a month later they had devel-
oped, at James's insistence, a morning routine to help
him to get dressed and ready for school on time.

Setting Up Routines

For many parents, getting the children up and ready on a
school morning and bedtimes are the most stressful times
of the day. Children sense their impatience and deliberately
begin to dawdle. Developing a clear routine helps the children to know what is expected of them, but it also helps
to keep the parent on track. If you feel that mornings,
evenings, or any other part of the day seem particularly
chaotic, then consider writing out a routine. If you have
older children, then they can be involved in the process.
For under-fives you will probably have to impose the
routine yourself. Work backwards from the last moment,
for example the time school starts in the morning, or the
time the lights go out at night. Write down all the things
the child has to do. With younger children, it is helpful to
draw little stick-man pictures to help remind them. Be realistic about how long the child will need and make sure you
allow enough time.

Routines also help to stop everything the child has to
do from turning into an area for discussion or negotiation.
When it's time to get dressed, it's time to get dressed. The
routine says so and therefore there is no argument. If
getting up in the morning is a movable feast, then the child
will try and negotiate to get the best deal every day. If the
child is allowed to stay in bed later on one day, then he will

expect an equally good deal the next day. If he doesn't get it the next day, he will be annoyed and confused. If he can negotiate a bit of flexibility, then he will try and do it every day and the boundaries will become more elastic. Every small thing will become a battle and you will end up stressed and in a mad hurry to get the children to school on time.

I am all in favour of giving children options and letting them make up their own minds, but there are certain things that may as well be non-negotiable, since they need to be done. Children have to get up in the morning, get dressed, eat their breakfast, clean their teeth and get ready for school, so why not set it in stone?

Make the Routine Clear

In the example of Jenny and James, I asked Jenny to write down the routine. This might seem ridiculously over-formal, like a school timetable, but it is really effective in working out how much time you need and in keeping the child (and you) on task. A friend of mine who asked for my advice was simply not leaving enough time to get her children dressed and breakfasted, and was leaving the house shouting at them every day. She hated getting up in the morning and was trying to stay in bed as late as she possibly could.

'You have a choice,' I said. 'Get up fifteen minutes earlier and have a calm morning or get up when you do now and shout.'

She couldn't do fifteen minutes, but she did manage ten. Now she only has to shout a bit!

Once the routine is solidly established, then you won't need to follow it so slavishly and you can be more flexible. After all, it's hard to keep up that level of military precision for long. However, if things begin to slip and you find yourself in a rush and going into reptile mode, then bring back the strict regime. Remember – your children will prefer you to be organised, calm and bossy than disorganised and hysterical.

Routines and Rewards

Within a good routine you can build in opportunities to give your children more positive attention. If they get themselves dressed and ready quickly, then you will be able to play with them, listen to them read, or simply have a longer, more leisurely breakfast, during which you are actually able to have a conversation. Make sure each task is completed before the child can go on to the next one. For example, if your children have to be dressed before they have breakfast, then that means they have put everything on including shoes, so that when it's time to leave all they need to do is grab their coat and bag.

As we saw with Jenny and James, rewards are very effective in supporting a new routine. At first, children will be resistant to the change and may need an additional incentive for a few weeks just to get things established. My wife has the rule that if my daughter gets dressed in time in the mornings, she gets her hair plaited. At the moment, this is a big incentive. It is also a good, logical consequence, that if you do what you are supposed to do on time, then you will get to have some quality time with your mother – and your hair styled the way you like it.

Routines with Competition

Young children are often quite competitive and you can use this to your advantage. I worked with a mother of four boys aged nine, eight, six and five. Mornings were a mad scrum to get the boys ready for school, during which there was a constant battle to see who could get the most attention from the mother. Don't forget that getting a few minutes of mum's attention is vastly more important to a five-year-old than getting to school on time. We turned getting ready in the morning into a race, in which all the boys had to help each other get ready. Their times were recorded and they aimed to beat their record every day. We also encouraged them to note down how much extra playtime they were having as a result of getting up more quickly. There didn't need to be an external reward, for the boys realised that if they hurried with the boring bits there was more time to have fun. The only thing we did have to watch out for was teeth-cleaning, which had become cursory. Their mother kept a set of toothbrushes and paste next to the kitchen sink where she could make sure they were used properly.

Routines During Times of Family Stress

At my school, when a family is going through a major trauma such as a relationship breakdown, the birth of a new sibling or moving house, we always emphasise to the parents the importance of keeping the family in tight routines. Major life changes will increase the amount of anxiety and fear children will feel about the future, and this often has a knock-on effect on their behaviour. Children can become more challenging, they will demand more attention and sometimes become clingy. Parents may also see the stress manifest itself physically in night-waking, bed-wetting and a change in eating habits. Children in these circumstances are overwhelmed by intense feelings that they can't name or describe and don't understand. If they are kept in a well-organised routine, they will retain a part of their life that, despite all the uncertainty, they can feel sure about. The temptation with children in crisis is to be more flexible and indulgent, but the opposite is so much better for them. Children in tricky situations need lots of reassurance and love, but they also like to know where they stand.

Rules

When I am talking to parents about rules, I often encounter some resistance. For some people, rules have a resonance of authoritarian teachers and school days, but what they are, simply, is one of the ways we communicate our values to our children. As a society, we are bound up in a myriad of rules, all with different levels of importance and for different situations. We have the rules of the country which tell us what we are not allowed to do. There are rules of the road, rules for communicating, rules for eating, rules for listening, for talking, for sitting, for speaking at home, for speaking at school, for speaking to our friends, for speaking to our grandparents and there are also rules that apply for people of different ages. If you were to count how many social and legal rules you follow during the course of a day, the number would be staggering.

As children grow up, we expect them to follow these rules. It is one of the endearing (and embarrassing) things about small children that they don't understand many of the social conventions. My daughter used to go up to complete strangers and ask them questions of a highly personal nature. By and large, she was able to get away with it because people are more tolerant of children, but as she grew older she needed to start to learn the rules of social interaction.

We consciously teach children many of these rules, such as eating with your mouth closed, and how to use a knife and fork. Children will also pick up a lot through school, through socialising with their friends and through playing. They will learn a huge amount from watching their parents. Children whose parents shout and swear in the car will have children who will shout and swear. Whether you like it or not, children will learn many of their values through the example set by their parents. Unfortunately, 'Do as I say, not as I do' doesn't cut much ice.

Using Rules to Improve Behaviour

When a behavioural issue arises in the family, it is often useful to impose an explicit rule to help the child know what he is not supposed to be doing. Let's take the example of brothers who fight all the time. To some extent, we want to encourage children to play-fight. They need to learn how to use their strength safely, how far to go before they hurt each other. However, what often happens is that one of the children ends up hurt and in tears. This is a useful time to impose a rule – one that is really simple and easy to understand, such as: 'be gentle' or 'don't hurt'. Once you have a rule, then you can teach the children what it means and how to follow it. With play-fighting, you could give the children a spoken or physical script they could follow when they are in pain. This could involve simply saying, 'Stop, that hurts!' or giving a series of taps to show things have gone too far. You can then ask the children to practise fighting and letting the other one know they are in pain. By doing this you are making it clear that there is no specific benchmark for what is too rough, beyond what is acceptable to the child concerned on that day. This helps the children to become more assertive, more sensitive and more responsible. When the children are fighting, you can simply remind them of the fighting rule.

The rule makes it so much easier than constantly having to resolve a bit of rough-housing that has gone too far. The parent will usually turn to the eldest child and say, 'How many times have I told you not to hurt your brother?' The child is not being taught what is acceptable, nor is the victim learning how to assert himself. Having a rule gives the parent a chance to give out some praise whenever it is being stuck to. 'Well done, boys, you are remembering the fighting rule,' is so much more effective than glibly saying, 'Be careful you two, we don't want it to end in tears.' To give weight to the rule you can have a reward to use when it's kept to and a sanction to use if anyone does get hurt. These can be clear and worked out in advance.

The Pile of Coats

I was at my friend Sally's house recently when two of her children, aged four and six, came back from a playdate. As they came through the front door they were taking their coats off. They said hello breezily to their mother and then headed for the television.

'Excuse me!' she yelled after them. 'Can you hang your coats up please?' Nothing happened.

'I said, hang your coats up.' The four-year-old started to cry.

Sally bent over and picked the coats up herself and put them on their pegs. 'Every day,' she said, 'they come through the door and chuck everything on to the floor. If I do manage to get them to pick things up, they fly into a rage and it takes them ages to do it.'

'What the hell can I do to make them do one simple thing when they come in, I mean it's so disrespectful, both coats are virtually brand new. And as for Jason, [her husband] he does the same thing.'

She was halfway into reptile mode so I made her a cup of tea while she spooned some orange gloop into the baby. We decided that there was going to have to be a rule, explicitly made and stuck to by everybody in the house. We kept it simple:

'No coat, No TV'.

Sally explained the rule to the children when she was feeling less stressed and made them rehearse coming through the door and putting their coats on the hook. She took some photos of them doing this and of them sitting watching television. She printed out the pictures and stuck them, at child height, on the door to the television room. The idea was they would come in, see the sign and remember the rule. Sally was to remind them of the rule in very simple language – 'Coat rule, please' – and she was to be ready with praise when they managed it.

The results were virtually instant. The children loved the rehearsal (they always do) and Sally only had to come in and turn the television off once because the coats were left on the floor. In a couple of weeks the children hung their coats up automatically, the rule became unnecessary and the photos could be removed. By making a rule, Sally was being explicit about what she wanted to happen and what the consequence would be if it wasn't followed. Her husband Jason has not improved at all.

Imposing a rule works whenever there is a bit of behaviour that needs to change. Once the behaviour has gone, then the rule becomes redundant. You only need to have an explicit rule when you have an explicit problem. Most rules are unwritten and can stay that way. You don't need to have a list of dos and don'ts stuck by the front door, but using rules is a great way of crystallising and tackling a problem.

Routines and Rules: A Summary

1 Children like routines. They make them feel safe and give them security in an uncertain world.

2 If a part of your day is particularly difficult or stressful with your children, think about devising a routine that will help everyone.

3 Write the routine down and display it in all appropriate places. It will help to keep you and the children on track.

4 When you start, stick to the routine. Once everything is settled, you can lighten up a bit.

5 If there is lots of uncertainty going on in your child's life, tighten up the routines.

6 Use rewards, especially praise, to give the routine a push.

7 Devise a rule when you have a particular problem.

8 Decide on the rule when you are calm, not when you are in reptile mode.

9 Explain the rule to the child and teach them how to follow it.

10 Use lots of praise, rewards and sanctions to help the child stick to the rule.

9

play for better behaviour

It may seem surprising to have a chapter about play in a book about behaviour, but I am convinced that the right sort of play will have a transforming effect on children.

For many parents, most of the playing they do with their children involves activities and most of this play is actually more like teaching. Looking at books, drawing, and playing games are of course essential, but in this chapter I will show how undirected play with the child taking charge will make an enormous contribution to his behaviour and development.

The longer I am in my job as a headteacher and the more I work with individual parents, I have come to realise the overwhelming importance of play. When I think back to my own childhood, some of the happiest and most powerful memories are of the hours I spent lost in play either with my siblings, with friends or alone. Time appeared to lose any meaning and the toys, usually soldiers in my case, took on a life that made them as real as I was. As a child, you have this astonishing power to control an army, run a zoo, look after a farm and give voices and characters to animals, dolls, teddies, cars and trains.

These playtimes are enormously important in children's development. Through play they develop their imaginations, learn to share, learn to negotiate, learn how to be in charge and how to let others be in charge. Play teaches children to develop empathy and sympathy: if you pretend to be someone else you get a sense of how they feel. Play allows children to learn to make mistakes and teaches them how to sort things out when they go wrong. Play gives children a chance to practise skills that they can transfer to the real world, such as getting dressed or cleaning the car.

I have often come across children who have not learnt to play properly. These children have spent too much of their early years watching television or plugged into a computer game. As a result, they have very poor social skills and have often developed serious behaviour problems. In my school, there is a sand tray in every classroom, so that even the year six children have an opportunity to play, and it is remarkable how much they get out of it. I recently visited a brand-new comprehensive school that had opened with only one year group. These twelve-year-old children were in a unique position, in that they had no older children to laugh at them and no younger children to be cool in front of. As a result, many of them spent their lunch breaks playing elaborate fantasy games involving role plays around *Dr Who* and *Star Wars*. It is depressing to think that this need to play in children is so often repressed by social constraints.

How Does Play Help Behaviour?

Small children exist in a shower of instructions. They have little control or understanding of the decisions that affect them, and most of the time things are done to or for them. As a result, children often try to take control of situations themselves. This is one of the reasons two- and three-year-olds turn into mini-dictators, as they try to wrestle control back from a world in which so many decisions are imposed on them. Children who know how to play and have lots of opportunities to do it are able to create a little world that they can run as they like, where they are the boss and everything happens exactly as they want it to. When parents regularly enter this world and join in, not as teacher or adult, but as a subordinate playmate, they will often see a remarkable transformation in their child's behaviour. By giving the child a short period of time when he is in charge, setting the agenda and telling the adult what to do, his power need is met and he is less desperate to take control the rest of the time.

This might all seem too simple and contrived, but if you give it a go it really does work.

The Power of Play
Clara, mother of Ben, aged four, and Francis, aged five, asked for my help. I went to visit the house to see

the boys in action. They fought continuously, but not in the rough-housing, play-fighting style you would expect (and want) to see in young boys. Very quickly, their fights would become vicious, and they would really hurt each other. They had begun to use toys as weapons which was a worrying development. Clara seemed to already be doing everything I would have suggested. She had a sticker chart on the wall in the kitchen and if they had three days in a row without fighting they would get to stay up half an hour later on a Saturday night. She had a naughty step which the boys were well-trained in using and she praised them a lot when they were doing the right thing. Clara was a working mother, in a high-powered job, but she had negotiated with her boss that she could leave work early on Mondays and Fridays, to be back by four o'clock. In the evenings and weekends, she was torn (as so many of us are) between needing some down time for herself and wanting to give the boys lots of attention. She usually found time to play some sort of board game with them, though she had recently stopped doing this because the loser had inevitably started fighting with the winner.

I felt that a lot of the boys' behaviour came from trying to squeeze a bit of precious extra attention from their busy mother and we discussed ways of making the attention she was able to give them more meaningful. We set up a system whereby she would spend ten minutes playing with each boy on five evenings a week. She wanted to commit to doing it every day, but I felt this was probably unrealistic. This playtime was not a reward, and they were to have it however bad their behaviour had been. They weren't allowed to play any win/lose board games, but otherwise it was up to the children to decide what to do.

It turned out that Clara wasn't really sure how to go about playing in the way I was suggesting so I offered to do a session for her with one of the boys. I had a play session with Francis at seven o'clock, after Ben had gone to bed. Taking a handful of plastic animals from the boys' farm, I put some water into a big saucepan and sat down on the kitchen floor. I got the kitchen timer down, set it for ten minutes and told Francis that when the bell went off, we would have to stop. I started getting the animals and making them jump off the edge of the saucepan, spiral high into the air and then land with a splash in the water. Francis started to join in, and though at first he was constantly looking to me to see if I approved of what he was doing and whether he was getting it 'right', I began to commentate on what he was doing without asking any questions or making any judgements. After a few minutes, he was bossing me about, telling the animals I was holding what they should be doing. I let him take the lead and gave him a two-minute warning when the time came. The buzzer went off with Francis in mid-flow and the animals in a high state of excitement. Francis was keen for me to go on. I said he was welcome to, but I was going to stop. He was annoyed and tried to cajole me into carrying on, but I wanted Clara to get used to making the play-time limited, so I wouldn't budge.

Clara started off by following my lead and played with Francis when Ben was in bed. When she played with Ben, she put Francis in front of the television. This was important because she didn't want her time with either boy disturbed.

I went to visit Clara four weeks later, and she reported that the boys were getting on far better. She had also started to play with both boys at the same time without them fighting for her attention. She said it had taken her a long time to get used to playing without taking control. After standing her ground a few times, the boys accepted the time limit of the play. Three months later, the relationship between the boys had transformed and, though they fought constantly, it was in a healthy, brotherly way without any of the nastiness that had been around before. They had found a way to get fair access to quality attention from their mother.

How to Use Play to get Better Behaviour

For some parents, playing with children comes easily. Perhaps their own mother or father used to play with them a lot and they remember how to do it, but for other parents, playing is hard.

Starting Off

First, get the children excited and intrigued, using lots of panto. 'Shall we have some special playtime now?'

Have a range of toys ready, get down on the floor and start playing with them. If you are not used to playing like this you will probably find it really strange and embarrassing. You might even want to do it when everyone else is out so you don't feel self-conscious. Your child will be intrigued and will come over and begin to watch. At first, he may be reluctant to join in because he doesn't know what he is supposed to be doing. After a bit, he will get the idea and start to join in. Once you have had a few play he will start to choose the toys and take the lead.

Don't Worry About the Outcome

Playing with children is not about the outcome, there doesn't need to be any product. Play is only about the process. If the child is building a wall out of Lego, you must resist the temptation to give a lesson on overlapping the bricks so it will pass health-and-safety regulations. As a teacher, I have to constantly stop myself from turning play into a lesson.

Let the Child be in Charge

This is your child's one moment in their busy adult-dominated day when they are completely in charge. You might want to set up the play to get the ball rolling but as soon as he has got involved, let him take over.

Don't Ask Questions

This is really hard to do, as we seem to be hard-wired to constantly ask our children questions. If you ask a question, you are very subtly taking control and manipulating the play. Also, if you are asking questions, children assume there must be a right answer, and they will try and find an answer to please you.

Commentate

As the child plays, say what you are seeing. 'The cow is flying over the farm, through Daddy's hair and into the water.' 'The blue train is coming down the track towards the red train, they have crashed!' If you get it wrong the child will correct you. Stick to commentary and try not to embellish with your own spin, such as: 'The cow is going into the water, I hope he can swim!' Or, 'They have crashed, I hope everyone is okay!' By doing that, you are immediately imposing your opinions and values into the situation and taking some control. Simply commentating works, however, because it stops you from asking questions or teaching, at the same time as validating whatever play the child is involved in. This is the child's time to be in charge and whatever they do is okay.

Don't Praise

There is no right or wrong way to do it, so don't praise the child. If you do, he will repeat the bits that you praised, because he wants to please you. If that happens then the play turns into a lesson.

How Much? How Often?

If you were able to have ten minutes a day of special play-time with each child you would see, over time, a big change in their behaviour. Ten minutes seems very little, but life is so busy that it is actually hard to find the time consistently.

Limit the Time

For this sort of play, it is really useful to limit the time. If you don't, you will find the play session will go on for ages and it will always end in a battle. The next time you play, the child will expect the same level of attention for the same amount of time. If you stop early next time, the child will feel short-changed and is likely to make a big fuss. Also, if you think the play session is always going to turn into a marathon then you will inevitably be more reluctant to start and they will stop happening with any regularity. It is far better to have frequent, intense play with your child than having a long playtime once a month. If the play is time-limited, you won't feel guilty when you bring it to an end. At first, it is very hard to end the play on time. You will probably be enjoying yourself and patting yourself on the back for being such a good parent. The child will also be desperate to keep it going. Be clear and firm about bringing the play to an end – after a time, he will get used to the time constraint and he will stop making a fuss.

Let the child know in advance how long the playtime is going to be. Even if he is too young to have any idea about time, you are letting him know there will be an ending. It can be useful to have an egg timer to turn over to show you are at the last minute and that you will stop when the sand runs out. Explain that, even though he will wish you could keep playing for a very long time, you are going to finish on time. By preparing him in advance like this he will find the ending less hard to cope with. Always give him a warning before the end, so he is not taken by surprise when it is time to stop.

What to Play?

Anything that gets the child interested. It doesn't usually matter much what you do, because one of the most exciting parts of the experience for your child is bossing you about.

Here is a list of things you could use to get the play going:

- Toy animals
- Teddy bears and soft toys
- Water in a sink or a bowl
- Kitchen equipment like whisks, funnels, spatulas and saucepans (this does not mean the play has to be about cooking, remember he is in charge!)
- Pretend your bed or an armchair is a car, let your child drive, see where it gets you
- Use the folds of your duvet or bedclothes – these can make an amazing world to play in
- Cardboard boxes
- Blocks or Lego bricks
- Sandpit

- Mud
- Garden
- Rugs spread over tables or chairs to make indoor camps
- Dried pasta
- Play-Doh

Avoid:

- Anything that involves skills such as cutting, drawing or sticking
- Games with rules, outcomes or winners such as cards or board games
- Books

Teaching your children, playing board games, kicking a football around and reading books with them are really important. We are rightly ambitious for our children and we want them to learn the skills to succeed in life. But for improving behaviour, making the child feel safe, developing imagination, empathy and understanding, undirected free play with the child taking the lead is the key. I promise.

Play for Better Behaviour: A Summary

1 Play is enormously important in the development of children's social, emotional and learning skills.

2 If young children have a chance to lead the playtime, with the adult taking the back seat, they will have less of a need to be in control the rest of the time.

3 Frequent, time-limited playtimes are better than long, occasional ones.

4 Don't intervene and try and teach when your child is playing. It is about the process, not the outcome.

troubleshooting guide

This section contains simple, practical solutions to a range of common problems that parents experience. It will not, of course, address every situation that arises, but by using the examples here and the ideas in the rest of the book, parents will be able to find successful solutions to most difficulties. I have included sections particularly relevant for older children such as homework and computers. For the parents of toddlers these issues will not yet be on the radar, but it is only a matter of time.

bedtimes and early risers

Bedtime

We know they're tired, they're flopping about the place like rag dolls, they burst into tears at the drop of a hat and they become incapable of doing anything for themselves. But, when the parent tactfully suggests it might be time for bed there are furious denials and more wild tantrums. It is tempting, but decidedly unhelpful, to point out to the child that his reaction is clear proof of his exhaustion.

Children resist bed and bedtimes for three reasons:

1. They lack the self-awareness to know that they are tired.

2. Refusing to go to bed and making a fuss gives them control and an opportunity for lots of attention.

3. They think they must be missing out on something.

Here is my plan for effective bedtimes.

1. *Have a routine*: As much as possible try to keep bedtimes the same every night. Give the child a warning that bedtime is going to start and then stick to the plan. Do things in a set order so that the child knows what is coming next.

2. *Make sure you have left enough time*: The worst bedtimes are when you have to do everything in a mad rush. This takes away all the fun and there is not enough time for your child to wind down properly. When you plan your routine, work out how long each part is going to take and work back from the time you turn the lights off. An hour from start to finish is a good benchmark.

3. *Make the room dark*: In the summer children will find it hard to drop off when there is light streaming in through the windows. Buy some blackout material to attach to the curtains, or invest in some extra blinds. It doesn't have to be pitch dark, but it must feel like night-time.

4. *Make bedtime at the same time every night*: If you are inconsistent about when you put your child to bed then he will try and push the boundaries. Why, he will think, should I go to bed at seven tonight when you let me stay up until nine last night?

5. *Make the end, the end*: Once you have kissed him goodnight and turned the light out don't let him try and hook you into giving him more attention. If parents give in to post-lights-off demands they are making a rod for their own back. Children will try anything, they are hungry, thirsty, they want another story, they want an extra kiss to get you back into the room. If you give in to one demand you will certainly get another and another. Be confident that you have given your child a happy, loving bedtime and refuse to bow to any more guilt-inducing demands.

6. *Use rewards and consequences*: If bedtime is becoming a problem then work out a reward to encourage the child. This can be difficult because he won't get it until the following day and so will not feel the same incentive as he will if he gets an instant reward. You have to be firm and consistent on this one.

7. *Change the bedtime*: If you are finding your child is going to bed and then failing to get to sleep, you may have to make bedtime later. Parents of older children rue the loss of that time when the house goes quiet and they can sip a glass of well-deserved wine in peace. Conversely, when children start school they will become extremely tired and you may need to make bedtime earlier.

Early Risers

One of the most draining things parents endure is the patter of little feet into their bedroom at some unearthly hour of the morning. Disturbed sleep is something all parents accept and learn to deal with, but children who consistently get up very early and wake the rest of the house can lead to levels of tiredness that can begin to have a corrosive effect on the whole family. The result of having a consistent early riser in the family is parents who are tetchy and on the verge of the reptile brain. Solutions to this issue vary, depending on the parents' attitude to having children in their bed and the age of the child.

Some parents are happy to be joined by one or more of their children during the night. Providing the child get into bed reasonably quietly and everyone is able to get back to sleep then there is not a major problem. Real difficulties arise when the child comes into the parents' room and demands attention, or when more than one child wants to snuggle!

Here is my plan to prevent consistent early rising.

1. *Buy a rabbit clock*: This is a child's clock that you set at the time your child is allowed to come into your room. Rather than an alarm going off, the rabbit's eyes open and his ears stick up in the air. Children can see the clock face even in a dark room and they don't need to be able to tell the time. Rabbit clocks are very effective and can be found in baby shops and children's catalogues.

2. *Put your child to bed later:* It may be that he is getting enough sleep, so try a later bedtime and see if there is an improvement.

3. *Cut down on nap times:* If your child is still having a nap, you may need to reduce it or cut it out altogether. Losing this precious peaceful time in the middle of the day is sometimes the price parents have to pay for a good night's sleep.

4. *Make sure the room is dark:* In the summer it can be light at half past four, so make sure the child's room is dark as dawn approaches. If a child comes into a lighter sleep at this time then he may wake up. Buy blackout material for curtains or buy some extra blinds. Get the child used to having a small plug-in night-light if he needs some light, rather than a blazing bulb in the corridor outside the bedroom.

5. *Praise:* If your child manages to stay in bed until the right time, give him lots of attention and praise. Make it worth his while.

6. *Use rewards and consequences:* If he can stay in bed until the rabbit clock pops up then how about a Smartie at breakfast? Keep it simple and stick to it for a couple of weeks. This is just a habit and it is breakable.

7. *Give no attention*: If your child does come in at night give him no attention, avoid eye contact and keep words down to a minimum. Pick him up and gently return him to his room saying, 'Back to bed, it's not morning yet.' He may well cry or scream to try and hook you in. Ignore this if you are able to.

8. *Use a stair gate*: If your child is still in nappies at night then there is no reason for him to leave the room. Put up a stair gate on his bedroom door to stop him coming out.

9. *Give him something to do*: At times children do wake up early naturally. If this happens occasionally then let him turn on the light and read or play with his toys quietly for a bit. Watch out for this becoming a pattern.

Bedtimes and Early Risers: A Summary

1 Ensure the child is not going to bed too early or getting too much sleep in the day.

2 Stick to your routines and make bedtime and getting-up time the same every day.

3 Tire your child out. If he isn't sleepy or he is waking up early take him out for more exercise. A run round the park with a football or a swim will help him to sleep longer and more deeply.

4 Make sure you give him lots of praise when he gets it right and try not to give him attention when he is supposed to be asleep.

5 Remember all children will find it hard to get to sleep at times and being woken early is an inevitable part of being a parent. Don't expect too much, it is only a problem when it has become a habit.

car journeys from hell

Car journeys with children can be hell. It is the worst feeling in the world being stuck in a traffic jam, or lost somewhere in the middle of the countryside, with one, two, three or more fractious children in the back.

Being in a car, for a child, is a desperately boring and unnatural experience. Young children spend most of their time charging around; suddenly we are expecting them to sit for hours at a time, strapped into a seat, unable to move. At the same time, they are often placed in close proximity to another equally bored and frustrated child. Young children also have no idea of time and distance and so they are unable to get a sense of how long they will be squashed into their seat.

This explains the chorus of 'when will we be there?' that starts five minutes after you have left the house and ends thirty seconds before arrival.

Long Journeys: Preparation, Preparation, Preparation

It is inevitable that children are going to whinge, fight, cry, shout, hit and bicker, so the essential thing for parents is preparation. If you get into the car for a long journey without being properly prepared you deserve all the aggro that you will inevitably get. Think of preparing for the children on a car journey alongside an essential like checking the tyres and filling up with petrol.

During the flap of packing – making final phone calls, trying to remember everything you need to do to get a family on the road, locking up the house – it is easy to overlook what you will need for a smooth journey. It is only when the first whinging begins that you realise you are woefully unprepared for what lies ahead.

Pack a bag before departure with a range of entertainment and food that will help to ease the pain. For long journeys there needs to be a wide range of activities and sustenance. On these occasions, forget good parenting – anything goes to keep the peace. However, it is important that this does not become the benchmark for every journey. With shorter journeys, children should be able to cope with a story tape or some music and they shouldn't expect to be fed biscuits and sweets every time they get into the car.

Praise in the Car
Don't wait until your children have started fighting before you interact with them en route. Give out lots of praise

from the start, noticing good sitting, sharing, manners and so on.

Seatbelts

I was once called by the parent of a four-year-old at my school. She was parked on the hard shoulder of the M4 and her son was running along the side of the carriageway.

'Please! Mr Taylor, will you come and help me?'

'No, I can't come out to the M4, get hold of him, pick him up and put him in the car.'

'But he won't sit still in the car.'

'Well, put him in his seat and strap him in,' I said.

'But he will cry!'

This is a somewhat extreme example, but it shows how parents can let the child set the agenda, because they are scared of the reaction they may have to deal with. When it comes to matters of safety there is no time to mess about. Children need to sit in their car seats and they need to get used to the idea. There is no scope for any argument or negotiation; simply pick them up and plonk them in. If they scream, then they scream. Soon, they will get used to the idea that you aren't going to back down, and the screaming will stop. If you have a child who gets out of his seatbelt then you can buy a device that fits over the release button and stops him from pushing it. There are times when the only way is to be tough and pitiless, and safety in cars is one of those moments.

How to Stop All Whinging, Fighting and Moaning on Long Car Journeys

1. Buy a packet of Smarties for each child and keep them in the front seat.

2. Tell them they are allowed to eat whatever is left when you arrive at your destination.

3. Whenever they whinge, fight or moan, ostentatiously take a Smartie from the miscreant's packet and eat it.

Car Journeys from Hell: A Summary

1 Praise good behaviour in cars.

2 Be prepared.

3 On long journeys, forget the rules, just get through any way you can.

4 Don't let children automatically associate being in a car with eating.

5 Don't negotiate when it comes to safety.

6 Use the Smartie technique. It works!

food and eating

Food is one of the most emotive issues for parents and can be the biggest cause of stress. There is wide, often angry debate about how children should be fed. My generation was brought up by parents who were born just before or during the war. Their attitude to food and eating was directly linked to those austere times when to leave food on the plate was an insult to the sailors who had risked their lives to transport the food to Britain. We were made to eat everything we were given and there was not much messing around with likes or dislikes. In these gentler times it would seem harsh to force children to eat something they don't like, or to continue eating when they are full just for the sake of an empty plate. On the other hand, food continues to have a sacred value in a world where people are starving and nobody wants to encourage children to be wasteful. I believe parents today, with thought, sensitivity and discussion, need to reach their own decision on where they stand on this issue. It will inevitably be something of a muddle, but once you have made a plan, stick to it.

In the meantime, we all wrestle with the day-to-day issues of children not eating enough of what we want them to eat, and eating too much of what we don't want them to eat. On top of this children are born with appalling table manners and it is a struggle to get them to eat in a way that is acceptable in polite society.

Feeding the Under-Fours

Young children are interested in getting food into their mouths using the fastest and most efficient method possible. This involves using their hands, a spoon when they can handle it, or getting the adult to do it for them. At this stage, the main concern of parents is making sure their child eats a balanced diet and begins to develop a bit of independence, without all the food ending up on the child's clothes or the floor. Parents also learn that, if the child eats well, particularly at teatime, he is more likely to sleep well. However, young children are not in the same regular habits as older children and their appetite seems to come and go. If your child eats virtually nothing at some mealtimes, don't worry too much and feel you need to force something down him. As long as he is generally eating well and putting on weight, there is not a problem. As children grow older, their appetite becomes more settled. I have found a tin of rice pudding is a good standby when you really think your child hasn't had enough to eat: it tastes sweet and contains lots of carbohydrates to give him energy and help him to sleep.

Under-fours will happily use their hands to eat and should be encouraged to do so with lots of finger-food. After a time, they will begin to get interested in using a spoon, although most of the food will be shovelled carefully over their clothes or on to the floor. Insist that your child wears a bib and stick with it. Often, children find bibs uncomfortable and restrictive but if you put it on for every meal they will get used to it.

For messy eaters, and children who have just started using a spoon, the most effective way to feed them is to do it in parallel. He has a spoon, you have a spoon, and while he has great fun smearing food all over his face and clothes, you surreptitiously slip spoonfuls into his mouth.

Don't get hung up on young children not finishing their meal; when they have had enough, they will stop. If you are going to give something sweet, such as a biscuit or some pudding to finish off, don't let them see it until they have had enough of their main course.

For children under three, always use a highchair with straps. Some children make a real fuss about sitting in highchairs, but it's tough. As with seatbelts in cars, there is no negotiating and once they are used to it, they will stop making a fuss. Highchairs are easy to clean, stop the child running off and allow you to keep an eye on how much they are eating. When your child is around three you will probably begin to dispense with the highchair, but don't put it back in the garage for a few weeks. If your child gets up from the table and starts to run around, you have the highchair ready to bring back into service if necessary. Often, the threat of the highchair is enough to keep small children in their seat.

Eat Your Greens: Persuading the Over-Fours to Eat Properly

With all the news stories about childhood obesity, parents often worry that their child is not eating enough of the right kind of food. Children scoff cakes, sausages and sweets, but some won't look at a piece of fruit or a vegetable. Mealtimes can be moments of high stress for parents, when they are constantly teetering on the edge of reptile mode, particularly if there is more than one child.

Snacking

Children do get hungry between meals and it is okay to let them have a snack in the middle of the morning and in the afternoon. If children are not eating properly at mealtimes, then the snacks are either too big or unnecessary. Don't let children help themselves to any snacks except fruit. If you want them to have a biscuit, then let them have it when you decide. This type of food is particularly satisfying to eat because of the fat and sugar content and children would munch them all day if you let them. Sugary food gives children an energy boost that quickly dies away, leaving them hungry again and demanding another biscuit. If you are firm about what and when your child can eat, you will be pestered less. Have a well-stocked fruit bowl and lots of dried fruit to pick at when they are hungry. If you are prepared to spend a bit of time and money buying a range of fresh fruit, you will be surprised at how much children will eat. If all that is on offer is a bruised, cotton-woolly apple and half a dried-up lemon left over from your gin and tonic, you are hardly offering a tempting alternative to junk food. Watch out for children taking one bite of a piece of fruit and then chucking it away. It is helpful to peel or cut it up for them.

Eat at the Table

Children can eat in front of the television as a treat or a reward, otherwise meals should be eaten at the table. Never get into the habit of letting children eat in their bedrooms.

Keep Portions Smaller

When you serve food to children, don't put as much food on their plate as you think they should eat. Hold back a bit and, if they finish, offer them some more. Children feel daunted when they are presented with a huge pile of food, especially if they think they might not like it or they are going to be forced to eat it all.

Prepare or Cook Vegetables Well

Try and be imaginative about cooking vegetables. If you serve over-boiled cabbage, don't be surprised if your children don't want to eat it. Try different vegetables and find out which ones your children like.

Fat is Good for Them

Don't be paranoid about your children eating fatty food. They need a higher proportion of fat in their diet than you do, to grow. You need only worry if they aren't eating anything else or they are becoming overweight. Cakes, crisps and biscuits are fine as long as children have them at the end of the meal.

Don't Get Too Hung Up About Food

As long as your child is eating some vegetables and fruit, they are probably fine. Turning mealtimes into a battle-ground is counter-productive. Sometimes parents are very strict about children eating everything on their plates. While I agree that children should not waste food, if they have had a good go at their meal, and they are full, then there is no point in going to war over a few mouth-fuls of pasta. If they are regularly leaving lots of food, make sure they are not eating too much between meals or filling up on pudding. Also consider serving smaller portions. You want your children to learn to enjoy food and see mealtimes as a pleasure. Whatever you decide is your policy on eating, make sure you think about it and you are consistent.

Make a Rule

If you think your child is really not eating enough fruit and vegetables, make a rule. For example, he has to eat some vegetables and fruit before he can tuck into the cakes, crisps and puddings. Put a small amount of the vegetable in front of him and say he must eat it before he can have any pudding. The best way to make this happen with children over four is to prepare their favourite pud, show it to them and say they can have it when they have eaten the stipulated amount of vegetables. If they won't eat the veg, then don't give them the treat. They will test you out a couple of times but when they realise you are serious, they will eat up. Over time, increase the amount of the fruit and vegetables you expect them to eat. This might seem really cruel, but if your child is not eating a proper diet then you need to take charge. At my school, we have a special unit for pre-school pupils with behaviour problems. When they arrive, the children have often never seen a vegetable, let alone tasted one. We are very firm with them. They have to eat some fruit before they have their toast in the morning and they must eat some vegetables before they can get down from the table and play. At first they resist like mad, but after a week, they get the idea.

'I Don't Like It!'

Before she got married and had Rose, Caroline had worked as a chef. She was a brilliant cook and her friends would all look forward to an invitation to dinner. Recently Caroline had given birth to a new baby and Rose had become very jealous. Rose, who was three and a half, seemed to be the only person who didn't appreciate Caroline's cooking. Caroline would beaver away in the kitchen producing another delicious, nutritious meal that she would place in front of her daughter. Without even trying it Rose would say,

'I don't like it.' When I became involved the situation was driving Caroline to distraction and she had pretty much given up cooking for Rose and was letting her live off frozen pizza and cake. As a result Caroline was feeling like a real failure. As we chatted I realised that Rose had used the food issue as a major attention-seeking strategy. Rose had worked out that by making a fuss about food, she could hook her mother into a fight, in which she could get lots of attention away from the baby. This was obvious because Rose had started to say, 'I don't like it,' even when she was given food she had specifically asked for. I was able to point out that Rose had found a particularly successful attention-seeking device because her mother was so passionate about food. We sat down and made the following plan to get Rose's eating back on track.

1. *When possible Caroline would try to sit with Rose and not be with the baby during mealtimes.*

2. *Caroline would go back to cooking for Rose, but initially she would serve smaller portions.*

3. *Caroline would insist that Rose tried a bit of everything.*

4. *Rose wouldn't have to eat everything on her plate, but she would have to have a pretty good go before she was allowed anything sweet.*

5. *Caroline would give Rose lots of praise.*

Caroline called me a week later to say there had been a huge improvement, she was sitting with Rose at mealtimes and giving her lots of praise. Rose was loving her food and had started helping with the cooking, giving her even more time with her mum.

Sweets

Sweets should be a treat, given occasionally. It is up to parents to decide how often and for what they should be given. If you offer children good fruit they will enjoy it as much as sweets and it will get them into better habits.

I am in favour of using sweets as rewards for good behaviour. As long as children don't get sweets all the time, then the child only needs a tiny amount. I recently set up pebbles in the jar to encourage my children to get dressed in time on school days. When they got ten pebbles they were allowed a square of chocolate after breakfast. On this scale food and sweet rewards are fine. It is only when children begin to associate being good with being fed that a problem can start to develop.

Food and Eating: A Summary

1 Try not to turn food into a big deal. Make a plan and choose your battles.

2 Young children are not always hungry when they're supposed to be. Don't worry if they sometimes have no appetite. As long as they are growing and eating some of the right things, they will be fine.

3 Eating between meals is okay, but you should be in charge of what and when your children eat. Snacks should mostly be fruit.

4 Don't get stressed about children eating every last morsel on their plate. If they are leaving food, make portions smaller.

5 If children won't eat enough fruit or vegetables, then make a plan, using praise and rewards, to persuade them to eat properly.

6 Make the effort to offer good quality fruit and well-prepared vegetables.

7 If children try something a few times, they will often develop a taste for it.

revolting table manners

What Can You Expect?

Parents often realise their children's manners need improving when they visit other people. They watch in horror as their children behave with all the grace of a chimpanzee, either on a playdate or worst of all, at the grandparents' house. The parents try desperately to hiss instructions and get their children to behave, without drawing too much attention to themselves.

'Say thank you.' 'Stay in your seat!' 'Eat up all your food!' But all this is usually in vain. Trying to suddenly improve your children's table manners when you are a guest is doomed to failure and humiliation. You end up furious with your children for embarrassing you, and furious with yourself for allowing your children to have got into such appalling habits. You can't wait for the visit to end.

One of the problems with children's table manners is knowing what is reasonable to expect, given the child's age. You might not expect a child under two to be saying please, but a three-year-old should easily manage it. You wouldn't expect a four-year-old to be able to use a knife and fork, but by the time a child is six, they should be pretty good at it. We tend to get stuck in a rut with our children's table manners and only realise we need to do something when we see them out in public, or we notice other children who are much better.

It is a mistake with table manners, as with all behaviour, to try and fix it in one fell swoop. Watch your children objectively over the course of a mealtime, and see how they ask for things, how they use their cutlery, how they sit and how they talk to each other. Try not to correct them, but make a mental note of what you would like to improve. Pick one thing that is particularly irritating, disgusting or rude and decide what you want to see instead. Before the next mealtime, get the children together and explain to them what you want them to do. Get them to practise it a few times and give them lots of praise for doing it right. When you call them to eat, remind them what you are going to be looking for. Use lots of panto to make it into a big deal. Whenever you see them doing what you want, describe what you are seeing and praise the child.

'Jonny, you said "please" when you wanted some water, well done!'

Try and notice it every time: 'Jonny, you said "please" when you wanted some more cake, well done!'

At first this will feel weird and artificial, but you will get used to it and it's a lot better than shouting. Keep this up for a few days until it has begun to be ingrained. Be very firm over the behaviour you want to change. If, for example, it's saying 'please', make sure they do it every time and don't give them what they want unless they say it. If necessary, you can use pebbles in the jar or sticker charts. When a child says 'please', they are allowed to put a pebble in the jar. When they have got twenty they can have a small and easily deliverable reward. When you are focusing on improving one bit of their manners, don't worry too much about other things. If you bombard your children with too many instructions and messages, you'll find that nothing much sticks.

Once you have made the first improvement, give it a few days to settle down and then you can set about changing something else.

Revolting Table Manners: A Summary

1 Children are born with appalling table manners. It is up to the parents to teach them how to eat politely.

2 Parents should set a good example with their own manners and eating habits. Children will copy what they see.

rude children

There are two types of rudeness, one from children who don't know any better and the other from those who are deliberately rude. In my experience, parents will often put up with levels of rudeness at home that then suddenly become a source of acute embarrassment when they are out and about. A friend of mine with a rude daughter got into the habit of saying please and thank you for the child.

'I want a cake!'

'Please can I have a piece of cake, Charlie?' said my friend, in a slightly babyish voice.

The cake is handed out, the child grabs it.

'Thank you, Charlie,' more baby voice.

The parent couldn't face correcting the child in public, knowing that she would have to deal with a full-on toddler tantrum – so she took the easy option.

In some ways, she was right. Trying to change your children's behaviour when you are a guest at someone's house is a disaster. You are in no position to use any strategies beyond bribery, cajoling and hissed threats of dire consequences when you get home.

I sometimes hear parents talking about their child's rudeness as though it is something innate that the child has developed and over which the parent has no control. This is not the case! Parents are totally responsible for their young children's manners, and it is up to them to decide what is and what is not allowed. If you allow your child to grow up being rude, you are doing them a huge disservice. The older they get, the harder it will be to change these habits. Rude adults are at a great disadvantage in life, for people won't like them, either socially or at work, but they are unlikely to discover the reason. When children are young, it is much easier for the adult to be in control and any bad habits that the child has picked up can be easily be changed.

The example the parents set to the child is of enormous importance. Parents who speak to each other and their children calmly and politely will have well-mannered kids.

Curing Rudeness

Setting Your Standards

The starting point when dealing with rudeness is to decide on your own standards. These should be appropriate for the age of the child. Remember: children under five are naturally pretty rude. They are still at a very egocentric stage and don't have much sense of how their behaviour may affect or come across to other people. Don't allow yourself to be overly influenced by other parents around you, who may put up with things which you consider unacceptably rude, or who you feel are far too strict. Bear in mind that whatever you decide is okay will be the standard you can expect from your children when you are out and about. If you feel embarrassed by your children when you go out, then you have set this benchmark too low.

Teaching the Basics

My own view is that children can learn from a young age, starting at around two and a half for early talkers, to start saying 'please' and 'thank you'. Once they are able to ask for things in simple sentences, I don't see why they shouldn't be able to stick 'please' or 'thank you' on at the end. I wouldn't make this into a crusade and I wouldn't deny them things because they haven't said 'please'. I would simply turn it into a game in which they get lots of praise whenever they do manage it.

'You said please!'

'Ooh! You said thank you!'

As children reach three and four, you can begin to be more insistent on good manners. When your child asks for something, remind them to say please and then praise them. Once you get into the habit of only letting them have things when they have said 'please', they will learn very quickly. The same goes for saying 'thank you'. You need to be really firm about this until the language is instilled in them.

Tone of Voice

Once your children are in good habits, you can then start working on the tone of voice they use, if it is grumpy or whiney. Tell the child you are going to imitate him, and ask him to listen to your voice. When you do this, the idea is not to be unkind or to humiliate the child, you are simply helping him to have a sense of how he is coming across. You can ham this up a bit and have a laugh about it with him, but the message is serious: this way of communicating is not on. You can then teach him the right way to talk, getting him to copy your tone of voice and practising a few times. Once he knows what to do, I find the expression, 'Right words, wrong voice', is a good reminder when they don't get the tone right.

If this general approach of demonstrating, teaching and praising good manners is not enough, then you may want to introduce some rewards and sanctions. Some children just get in the habit of being rude. They pick up their tone from their friends and siblings and get stuck with it.

Stay positive, expect change and tell him what you want to hear and see. Have a reward for politeness that your child can work towards. Make the focus on what you want them to do, not on what they are doing wrong. There is a real danger, when correcting manners, of parents turning into nags. Have a simple sanction for whenever the child is rude, but make it very clear in advance what is not acceptable. You can use five minutes time out or five minutes off screen time, whatever is easier to manage. Make sure you follow through with the sanction whenever you get the undesirable behaviour.

When children are rude to us it puts us into reptile mode and we often become angry and snap back. Unfortunately, this can often make things worse and our reaction makes the behaviour more likely to happen again next time. Having a plan ready will help to deal with rudeness calmly and successfully.

At my school, we have a number of pupils from very deprived backgrounds who have no social skills whatso-ever. They come to us with no idea about saying 'please' or 'thank you' and constantly use an aggressive voice. With lots of training we teach them to use the right words with the right tone of voice. We have a standard that we demand they keep to, we reward them when they get it right and we have a consequence when they get it wrong. These children can learn to be polite and so can your chil-dren. What is required is the clear setting of a standard and a bit of determination. Your children will 'thank you' for it one day.

Rude Children: A Summary

1 Take a few minutes to decide on what your standards are when it comes to manners. Given your children's ages, what do you think is reasonable to demand?

2 Speak politely to and around your children, as they will learn by example.

3 When they are old enough, insist that your child says 'please' and 'thank you' appropriately.

4 Work on their tone, and teach your child how to say things as well as what to say.

5 Children are often not deliberately being rude, but they don't realise how they are coming across so it can help to mimic how they sound.

6 Don't put up with rudeness. You are in control, you set the standard. Never let children get what they want if they are being rude.

7 Give lots of praise when you hear good manners.

8 Use rewards and sanctions as back-up to help you teach your children to learn good manners.

other people's children

'How was he?' the mother asks, slightly anxiously, collecting her son from a playdate.

'Oh, he was lovely, so polite,' you say through gritted teeth.

'Great,' she says, 'let's do it again soon.'

'Er, yes, let's.'

What you really want to say is: Your son is the biggest brat I have ever come across in my life. He is rude, spoilt, charmless, selfish and greedy. He has no idea how to behave, he has broken my children's toys, bullied my youngest daughter and trashed their bedroom. He will never cross this threshold again and I am considering moving house, school, possibly even country to avoid having to see him.

It is inevitable that your child will become friends with children you could do without seeing. This goes on throughout their lives and can become even more of a problem when your children are teenagers.

Children who visit on playdates may come from totally different backgrounds, where the parents have values that don't coincide with yours. This can be a minefield, because people are incredibly sensitive about their own children, and may take enormous offence if you give the impression that they are anything but absolutely perfect.

My House, My Rules

Most of the time, you can ignore low-level brattishness from visiting children. They may not say 'please', they may grab at the food or lack charm, but they are not your children and, unless they are really causing mayhem, they are not your problem. Remember that young children get excited and anxious when they are on a playdate so they might easily forget how to behave. Bear in mind, too, that it might not be the malign influence of your little guest, but the general excitement of the playdate that has caused a falling-off of standards in your home.

If things get so bad that the visitor is being actively rude, upsetting your children, refusing to do what he is told or being unsafe, then you will need to take action. After all, you have been left in charge of the child, so you are the boss and it's your rules that count.

You don't want your own child being adversely influenced by the visitor; nor should you allow your standards to drop dramatically to accommodate him. Also, bear in mind that it is not your responsibility to 'sort him out' and return him to his mother as a buffed, perfect specimen of charming humanity.

Try to Find Something to Like About Your Visitor

If you find the visitor particularly loathsome, you will probably unconsciously project your feelings towards him. He will become aware of your feelings, which will make him even more unlikeable. Try to find something to like about him, even if it's just discovering you like the same football team. We do it at my school and it makes a real difference to building relationships with hard-to-like children.

Praise

Whenever he does the right thing, praise him. 'Lovely manners, Jack,' or 'Good sharing, Jack,' and so on. This will help him to understand the things that matter in your house.

Tell Him the Rules

'Jack, we have a sharing rule here.' 'In this house you have to do what an adult says first time.'

Do this in a calm, friendly way and avoid sounding hectoring, cross or nagging. What you want is for him to toe the line, not have a horrible time. If he ignores you, then take him aside, away from any audience, get down to his level and repeat the instruction in a firm, no-nonsense way. You could add, 'I don't want to have to call your mum and ask her to take you home.' Immediately afterwards, try and catch him doing the right thing and heap on the praise.

'Jack, you did what I said first time!'

If he carries on being really out of order, then give him one more warning and then call his parents. I would only envisage doing this in extreme circumstances. If your child is under eight, then the friendship with the child will probably not be that firm and you can probably get away with not inviting him again. If your child is older and is adamant that he wants to play with his badly behaved friend, then go ahead, but do a little planning in advance. The techniques you use will also be useful for cousins and the children of close friends who you are inevitably going to have round, however awful they are.

Planning for Nightmare Visitors

If you know that your visitors are going to make trouble when left to their own devices, then think in advance about some activities that are easy to manage and that you know they will enjoy. If your visitor can't cope with losing, then avoid competitive games; if your visitor has lots of energy then take him to the park. Have dressing-up clothes or puppets ready if they like putting on a show, or dig out the paints and paper if they are into art.

When they arrive get them in for a quick pep talk about what the rules are and what you want to see.

'Okay, guys, the rules are:
■ If a grown-up asks you to do something, do it first time.

■ Play together nicely with lots of good sharing.

■ Tidy up at the end.

■ I want to see you being kind to each other, keeping calm, not leaving anyone out and enjoying yourselves.'

You can set up a little reward system that will help them to follow the rules and keep the lid on the hyped-up behaviour. Decide what you want to see and have some Smarties ready for the children to earn.

If the children end up fighting, reward co-operation. If they get over-excited and ignore you, then reward them when they do follow instructions first time. If they are rude, then reward politeness.

At the end of the playdate, how honest you are able to be with the parent collecting will depend on how well you know them. You can be more candid with close friends and family, but never underestimate how sensitive people can be about any criticism of their children.

When the parent is there and their child is behaving appallingly, it is rather awkward and unless you know them really well there is not much you can do. Praise your own children for doing the right thing and feel smug about what a brilliant parent you are.

Other People's Rude Children: A Summary

1 It is not your job to train other people's children, just to look after them.

2 Don't worry too much about low-level bad behaviour.

3 If the visitor is going too far or being unsafe give a firm warning.

4 With regular guests, plan in advance. Since you know what is likely to happen, pre-empt it by being prepared.

5 Have a reward system ready to encourage the behaviour you want.

6 Praise good behaviour.

7 Try not to get involved in the children's minor squabbles. It's good for them to learn to resolve conflict. Acknowledge the feelings and then ask them to deal with it. 'You're both quite cross, do you think you can sort it out yourselves?' They usually can.

sibling rivalry

One of the most exhausting and stressful things about being a parent is having to sort out squabbles between children. This can turn into a corrosive situation in a family when two children really don't get on or begin to actively dislike each other.

We have a dream of a harmonious family in which everyone loves each other dearly, supports each other and sorts out disputes in a grown-up, sensitive way. The truth is rather different. Inevitably, members of a family get on better with one person than another and this will continue into adult life.

When it comes to siblings who don't get on, remember there are many important factors that you can't change. The sex of your children and their positions in the family relative to each other set the tone for sibling relationships, as do the children's personal temperaments and interests. Bear in mind that it is a good and healthy for children to have squabbles and fights. They need to learn how to fall out, and then make up, as a part of growing up. When the siblings are constantly at each other's throats or the arguments are getting really nasty then you need to take some firm action and use my six-point plan.

While we are on the subject of siblings, we need to accept that our children are not necessarily going to be best friends with each other. What we want is for them to be able to get on well, sort out disputes without running to their parents for help, respect each other's space and learn to share and look out for each other.

Six-Point Plan for Happy Siblings

1. *Make the plan*

   In a quiet moment in the evening sit down and think about what is causing the most problems between your children. What do they do to one another? How do they react and what is the outcome? Now you've done that, think what you would like to see instead. Don't aim for total peace and harmony, it's unrealistic. Just pick one area when they are most at each other's throats and work on that. You will often find that, if you can get improvement on one thing, such as sharing toys, there will be a knock-on effect into other areas of behaviour.

2. *Teach the plan*

   Sit the children down and explain to them what you think the issues are and what you see happening. Don't turn this into a telling-off, simply tell them what you see and hear. Then tell them what you want to see instead. Give lots of descriptive praise whenever you see them doing it. If your children can't share, show them how to do it and teach them the language they can use. 'Please may I borrow that?' 'May I have a go after you?' 'I'm sorry, but I was playing with that first.'

3. *Rehearse the plan*

Take them through a few scenarios in which they imagine an argument, show them how they could sort it out, then get them to act it out for you. Use lots of panto when you do this and give out loads of praise. This is good fun for the children, but it will also help you to crystallise what you are looking for.

4. *Reward the plan*

Plan a simple reward that you can give them every time you see them doing what you have asked. Make sure they get the reward instantly and that it is shared between them. Pebbles in the jar is very effective for this as it is easy to administer and children like the physical act of putting a pebble into the jar. When they have got a pre-agreed amount, they can receive a small reward, together. At first you may feel they are manufacturing situations in order to get a pebble, but this is no bad thing as it encourages teamwork. They are beginning to be nicer towards each other and soon this behaviour will begin to be habitual. After a few weeks, you should be able to stop the rewards and rely on praising them when you see them playing properly.

5. *Have a sanction*
As part of the plan, have a simple, small consequence that you can use whenever they slip back into the old ways. You could send them to their room, to the naughty step or you can take away a privilege such as some screen-time. Make sure the sanction is easy to administer and can be done instantly.

6. *Keep praising*
Keep going with the rewards for three or four weeks at the most. By then the behaviour will be ingrained, but always keep on using lots of descriptive praise whenever you see them doing the right thing.

The Patch-Up Place

The idea is to have a space that children associate with solving problems. When they have a disagreement, they go there together and patch things up.

Choose a small area in the house as your patch-up place. This could be a piece of carpet, the hall, a corner of the children's bedroom, and ideally it should be away from the main living area of the house so that the rest of the family is not disturbed. Explain to the children that whenever they are arguing they must go to the patch-up place. Practise it with them a few times and teach them the language to sort things out. 'I'm really cross because you borrowed my toy without asking,' 'You woke me up,' 'You pulled my hair.' Teach them to state their case and then to work out how they can sort things out. When they go into the patch-up place, they are not allowed to hit each other and they have to stay there until the problem is solved or they have truly reached stalemate. Don't expect your children to know how to sort out an argument; they need to be taught this skill. It may help to put a copy of the rules up in the patch-up place to remind the children what to do. If your children start to argue when you are out of the house, simply send them to a temporary patch-up place until they have sorted it out. 'Okay, you two, stand under that tree, discuss the problem and come back when you have sorted it out.'

Rules for the Patch-Up Place

1. No hurting.

2. Keep voices calm.

3. Each take it in turn to explain your side of the story, don't interrupt.

4. Each take it in turn to say what you want to happen.

5. Agree on a solution.

6. Apologise if you need to.

You can also add on:

7. Tell Mum or Dad if you have sorted out a problem or if you have got stuck.

8. Give yourselves a reward.

The patch-up place is very effective once children have learnt how to use it for the following reasons:

- It takes children away from the problem and often serves to trivialise it.

- It helps them to realise that by arguing they are wasting their own time.

- They will stop arguing as a way of getting your attention.

- When children go to the patch-up place they are focusing on the solution rather than the problem.

- They learn to sort out their problems rather than rely on you to help them.

- They learn a language of reconciliation and peace-making that they can use elsewhere.

In the early days, the siblings may need extra help from you with resolving arguments, but don't get involved until they have tried to find a solution among themselves. When they have learnt how to use the patch-up place, allow them to involve you only when they have reached a real stalemate. When this happens, do still let them do most of the talking, help them to find the nub of the issue and then ask each of them, 'What do you want to happen?' They will usually come to a conclusion fairly quickly.

Once they have had some practice, they will become so good at sorting out disagreements that they will do it quickly and automatically and will only need the patch-up place in exceptional circumstances.

When the argument is resolved, ask them to come and explain to you how they got there. This will allow you to ensure the solution is equable and one child isn't dominating proceedings. It also means you are able to give them praise and attention for sorting the matter out rather than having a fight.

It is also important for children to see how parents argue and how things get resolved. If they see you screaming and throwing plates then they will see this as an acceptable way to behave. At my school, the adults deliberately argue in front of the children to show how a disagreement can be resolved happily and without the swearing, violence and aggression that our pupils have been exposed to at home.

Warring Siblings
I got a phone call a couple of years ago from Lisa, a parent who had come to one of my talks. She was very concerned about her two children, Jack, who was seven,

and his five-year-old sister, Melissa. They had begun to argue whenever they were together and Melissa's behaviour started to decline. She became vindictive towards her brother and seemed to delight in getting him into trouble. Mornings were the worst. The children squabbled over trivialities at the breakfast table and they were both acutely aware of how much attention the other was getting.

I made some suggestions as to how Lisa could make things better, but I also tried to keep her goals realistic. The aim was for the children to stop antagonising each other, not to become best buddies.

To begin with, we made a rule for the children to follow at mealtimes. It was: 'We all talk politely at the table.' I wanted to keep it short so Lisa and the children would remember it. I then asked Lisa to teach them what we meant. They acted out how it would sound if they were rude to each other, and what it sounded like when they were being polite. She took some photos of them being polite and printed the best one out on card with the rule written above it and a reward underneath: 20 pebbles = puppet show with Mum. Lisa drew a little stick man picture of her and the children doing a puppet show. This sheet was propped up at the end of the table at every mealtime to remind everyone what was going to be happening. Lisa put some pebbles in a black velvet bag and every time she saw the children being polite they both got to put a pebble into a jam jar.

I stayed to watch teatime on the first day, and the children tried really hard. Lisa was still in critical mode at times, but the children were quick to remind her whenever they were being polite, and by the end of the meal, they had earned five pebbles each, halfway to a puppet show! I had a quick chat with Lisa afterwards and she said it was the most harmonious tea they had had in a long while.

'I can't see it lasting more than a couple of days though,' she said.

I was concerned that if Lisa felt like this then her prophecy would become self-fulfilling and I challenged her. I pointed out that the children were caught up in a negative pattern, but the pattern was breakable. They would not be able to do this without Lisa staying positive, praising and rewarding.

A week later, Lisa called me to say the children were being much more polite to each other. However, she felt that a lot of the time they were only saying things in order to get the rewards and that they were manipulating the whole reward system.

I said this was great news! I explained that the children didn't have a habit of being nice to each other and needed to learn the skill. At first, of course, the whole situation was manufactured, but the children were being nicer to each other and that was the most important thing. Lisa also admitted that though she felt the whole thing was completely artificial, mealtimes had become far more pleasant. This was the thing I wanted her to hang on to. The idea was that the children would eventually lose the habit of being horrible to each other and the polite, positive, supportive behaviour would become ingrained in them. I also wanted Lisa to become used to dishing out lots of praise.

I spoke to Lisa again three weeks later. The children had kept up the improvement, and they had also begun to be nicer to each other away from the table. Melissa had gone back to being angelic, but the biggest change was in Jack, who had become much more loving towards his sister and had begun to look after her in a way he never had before.

I suggested Lisa continued with the rewards for one more week. This worried her because she thought the children might slip back into their old habits. I explained that the behaviour was ingrained and the children would accept not getting a reward because they would also have noticed and appreciated the change. All Lisa needed to keep things on a positive footing was to keep going with the 6 to 1 strategy, focusing on praising the children whenever they were being polite or playing well together.

Sibling Rivalry: A Summary

1 There are lots of factors parents can't change, such as gender, position in the family and temperament. Not all siblings are going to be best friends, however much we might want it, but parents can expect siblings to be kind, supportive and caring towards each other.

2 Much of sibling rivalry comes from the children vying for limited parental time. The more parents dive in to sort out squabbles, the more children will see arguments as a way of getting attention. Wherever possible, children should be taught to solve problems by themselves and given lots of praise whenever they manage it.

3 If your children are not getting on, don't hope to change things overnight. Choose one troublesome time of day and focus on that.

4 Teach the children how you want them to treat each other and get them to rehearse it.

5 Do lots of activities your children enjoy doing together.

6 Teach your children to use a patch-up place when they have an argument.

7 Praise them when you see them playing well, co-operating or sorting out a disagreement.

8 Use rewards to help break down established patterns of behaviour.

well-intentioned grandparents

Many parents will notice, often to their surprise, how close their own parents get to their children. For grandparents, it is a new and liberating experience to have the rapport, the love and the close connection with their grandchildren without the burden of responsibility that is felt by parents.

It doesn't always work out this way. There are some stereotypes of grandparents that have arisen out of painful truth. The overbearing mother-in-law who feels it is her duty to interfere in her grandchildren's upbringing is still causing tensions in many families. This situation is made more complicated by the resonance that our own parents and upbringing still have for us. We continue to do things to please our parents even if they are long-dead and gone, as the memory of our own childhoods whether good, bad, or indifferent, stays with us for ever.

When families get together, individuals tend to return to their traditional roles and place in the system and everyone behaves as they are expected to. When a family member behaves outside his prescribed role, such as the 'lazy one' jumping up and doing the washing-up, other family members will subconsciously push him back to his true position to ensure everyone feels comfortable and safe. 'Miracles do happen! Look who's doing the washing-up!' Such talk has the inevitable effect of encouraging the 'lazy one' back on to the sofa.

This social squeeze that is imposed on us by families also impacts on the relationship between children, parents and grandparents. Parents become desperate for their children to behave around their grandparents, because they are keen to please them and show what a good job they are doing. Grandparents can be critical of the way their children are parenting because they are keen to retain the authoritarian, adult role.

Grandparents Who Interfere

Parents are enormously sensitive to any criticism of their children and even more so when it comes from their own parents. It can be infuriating to hear grandparents say, 'We wouldn't have done it like that,' or 'Don't you think it's time these children were in bed?'

Grandparents can also develop a rather skewed, rose-tinted view of the past in which their own children were sleeping through the night at two weeks, were potty-trained by a year, never cried and had impeccable table manners by the time they were two.

I believe there is an equation that says: the more involved the grandparents are with the children, the more right they have to have their say. If you are lucky enough to have grandparents who look after your children, then, to a large extent, you have to allow them to do it their way. This also gives them a right to complain about them, in the same way that you would expect feedback from a nanny or a babysitter. The worst sort of criticism is that which comes from a grandparent who sees the grand-children twice a year at Christmas and birthdays.

Grandparents can also be critical about the amount of food children are allowed to leave on their plates. If you have worked out your own plan for mealtimes, and you have rules about how much your children need to eat and how much they are allowed to leave, then you can explain it to your parents or in-laws. They may not agree, but after all they are your children, and a plan is a plan. Once they know this, most grandparents will back off a bit. If it is getting intolerable, then you may want to feed your children before you get to the grandparents' house or let them know in advance that you will bring your own food. When you get there, why not say that you will do the cooking and then, if possible, get your husband or wife to distract them.

'I don't think I've seen round your garden for ages ...'

'Do you think I could possibly have another look at your coin collection?' etc.

As people get older, they often become less tolerant, and many elderly people suffer from hearing loss or de-teriorating health and spend much of their time in some discomfort. This can make them bad-tempered and easily irritated by small, noisy children charging round the place. Be thoughtful. If your children are being a nightmare, take them out to give everyone a break. Remember that however wonderful you know your children to be, the shine does begin to wear off after a while, even for the most doting grandparent.

Try not to let your children trash the house too much and make sure you clear up before you go. Your children are unlikely to be perfect, however much you want to show your parents or in-laws what a wonderful parent you are, so don't get too hung up on minor bits of behaviour. Also, bear in mind, if your children behave badly and embarrass you, there is little scope for you to teach them manners or change their behaviour when you are out and about or with company. You need to tackle this behaviour in the comfort of your own home.

Well-Intentioned Grandparents: A Summary

1 Be mindful of your own feelings when it comes to your relationship with your parents.

2 The more the grandparents are involved with your children, the more they should be allowed to comment.

3 If there is a particularly stressful part of visiting grandparents, such as mealtimes, think about how you can change things to make life easier.

4 Grandparents may have a rosy view of the past. Take it with a pinch of salt!

5 Respect the fact that older people often have ailments that leave them in discomfort. Be sensitive and tolerant.

6 Make sure your children clear up the mess they have made before they leave.

whining

Some children never do it, while others never seem to stop. Nothing that happens to them is ever quite right and they constantly focus on the negatives in any situation. This is particularly draining for adults and it feels like it happens more when you are tired.

When dealing with whining, the first thing is to eliminate the physical factors. If your child is not getting enough sleep, then he is more likely to whine. Consider whether he is going to bed eary enough, or whether he would benefit from a lunchtime nap. This also applies to older children. A quick twenty minutes, even for six- or seven-year-olds, can work wonders, especially if he has got into the habit of waking early.

Check that your child has eaten enough. Children under eight can find it hard to go between meals without some sustenance, so allowing your children free access to bananas and apples can often have a positive impact on whining. Finally, make sure your child is drinking enough. Give him a good-size cup at mealtimes and make sure he finishes it before getting down from the table.

One of the main reasons for whining is that as an attention-grabbing technique, it's a sure-fire winner. Children learn that whining is a good way of getting some one-to-one attention.

'Muuuuuum, please can you help me with my shooooes?' It is very tempting to go for the quiet life by doing his laces for him, but it often leads on to something else:

'Muuuuuum, I can't find my coooooat.' By judicious use of whining, children are able to get themselves lots of attention by getting us to baby them. Parents may often notice this when a younger sibling or baby has just arrived. However, whenever a parent responds to whining, they make the behaviour more likely to happen next time.

The difficulty with whining is that, for whatever reason it starts, it can soon become a habit. For some children, whining seems to become the default way of communicating with adults. If you have a child who whines too much and you have ruled out the physical factors, then you can start work on the behaviour using the following simple formula.

1. Let the child know what the whining sounds like, and do an imitation of the noise he makes. Get him to do a demonstration back so he knows exactly what you are talking about. It can be helpful to make a joke out of this, but remember you are not doing it to humiliate or tease them.

2. Get him to say something in Whinese and then repeat it in a normal voice. Often, the whining is so ingrained that the child doesn't notice he is doing it.

3. Explain that you won't help him when he uses the whiny voice and have a cue you can remind him with, such as: 'I'll do it when you use the right voice,' or 'Remember to use the right voice,' or my own favourite, simply: 'Voice.' Don't ignore the whining. Younger children won't understand why you aren't reacting to them and they will get upset and go into reptile mode.

4. When he does use the whiny voice, never do what he wants you to do. You will often be in such a habit of being hooked in by whining that you find you have done what he wants without really noticing. After all, if children didn't get what they wanted from whining, they wouldn't have developed the habit in the first place.

5. When he does use the right voice, be ready to leap on him with lots of praise. 'Lovely voice,' 'What a nice way to ask!'

6. If you need to, use simple, easy to administer rewards and sanctions to back up the praise.

Whining: A Summary

1 Eliminate the physical factors that may be contributing to whining.

2 Be aware that whining is an attention-seeking technique. If it didn't work, children wouldn't use it.

3 When you give in to whining, however tempting, you are making it more likely to happen again.

4 Work on the formula to break the habit.

homework

Schools seem to start giving children homework at a ridiculously early age. This often stems from parents who have become worried that their child is being left behind by their high-flying peers in other schools. Some parents see their friends' children doing piles of homework every night and think they must agitate for more homework in their own children's school.

Recent research assessed by the US Center for Public Education suggests that young children get little out of their homework and, in many schools, homework is a token gesture from the teacher in order to appease parents. For what it's worth, I don't think there is much point in children doing homework before they are ten. I would far rather children were spending their spare time playing than sitting at the kitchen table doing an hour's work on top of the five they have just done at school. Young children get far more from messing about with their toys and their siblings than they do out of plodding through a photocopied worksheet. Of course it is helpful for children to practise a little reading and brushing up on a bit of mental arithmetic won't do any harm either. I would say, however, if in doubt, let them play.

Nevertheless children are going to have to do homework at some stage and it is important that you get them into good habits for the future.

How to Help Your Child to Help Himself

Persuading Children to Do Homework
Don't leave it to the last minute. If the work is set a few days before it needs to be handed in, make sure it is started early. Do a little bit each day or split the work into a couple of manageable chunks.

Have a Set Place for Doing Homework
With younger children this will probably be the kitchen table as they will need fairly constant supervision. Older children can do the work independently in their bedroom. Never let children do homework in front of the television!

Have the Right Equipment to Hand
Make sure you have a box or a pot stocked with pencils, a rubber, a sharpener, a ruler, some coloured pencils, scrap paper and scissors. If your child has problems with his grip, buy pencils shaped like triangular prisms which will encourage him to use the correct tripod grip. Older children will need a proper desk and a chair at the right height. Children should not work on the floor, on their laps, or on the sofa. They have to be able to sit in

the right way for the sake of their posture and their handwriting.

Reduce Noise and Interference

Children need to be able to work without being disturbed. Encourage them to do homework when younger siblings are in bed, or let the little ones watch television while the older children do their homework. Some children like to work to music, but this should be quiet and unobtrusive.

Find the Right Time

Work out when is the best time of day for doing homework. Younger children will need support and encouragement, so make sure you are available and not charging around making tea and sorting out the other children. The best time will also depend on the temperament of your child. Some children are very productive first thing in the morning, while others work well in the evening.

Reward Them

Let the child give themselves a little treat when they have finished their homework. This could be playing on the computer, watching a bit of television or getting some attention from you. Never let them have the reward in advance.

Don't Do It For Them

If your child really doesn't get it, you can help a bit or talk to the teacher. You don't want to foster dependence and 'learnt helplessness' in your child. There is a danger that your child will make himself unable to do his homework as a way of getting a bit of extra parental attention. Give a short explanation at the beginning if he is stuck, and then let him get on with it.

Set little targets to help him stay on track. 'When you have done the first four, let me know and I will come and check.' You *are* giving him attention, but it is as a reward and on your terms.

Too Much Homework?

Talk to the teacher. Often they will be happy to let your child do less. Many teachers, particularly of younger children, aren't big fans of homework anyway and will be happy to reduce it a bit.

Homework Refusers and Whingers

Many children hate doing homework and will make a real fuss about it. This can turn into a constant, exhausting battle in which everyone gets really fed up and the homework is done sloppily, late and under duress. If your child refuses to do homework then you will need to tighten up on procedures.

1. Explain that it has got to be done, whether he likes it or not. He can have a battle about it every evening and it can take ages, or he can get down to it and it will be done much quicker. He will soon realise that he might as well go quietly.

2. Have a set time and place to do it, agree this in advance and stick to it. 'We are going to do your homework on Wednesday evenings the moment you get back from school.'

3. Have a reward that he gets for finishing it, and keep it small and manageable. 'When you have done your homework you can watch twenty minutes of television.'

4. If the child has failed to finish his homework, then he needs to stay at the table until it is done and he doesn't get to watch his twenty minutes of television.

5. If you are firm and unbending, he will get into the habit and he *will* do it.

6. Reward non-whinging. Often the whinging is the worst bit about doing homework. Set your child a target so that if he gets down to his homework without making a fuss, he can get a reward. Pebbles in the jar works well for this.

Homework must be done! This is one of those areas of parenting where there is no point in negotiating. Getting your child into good habits will save you both a lot of trouble in the future.

Homework: A Summary

1 Get your children into good homework habits. It is going to be a feature of their lives for the next twelve years or so.

2 Make homework routine: have a set time and place for it.

3 Set a small reward for completion of homework without whinging.

sport and games

Divas and Dictators Who Can't Lose

Sport is about winning, and children recognise this. However much we tell them that it's the enjoyment and the taking part that are most important, they think this isn't true. When children watch a football match on television, they see the winners celebrating and the losers looking miserable and even crying. At the post-match interviews you don't hear players saying: 'I know we lost, but I really enjoyed the game and it was great fun having the opportunity to be a part of it.' Yet this is the attitude we expect from our children. On top of this, children seem to be naturally competitive, perhaps partly caused by the perennial fight for parental attention. When children lose, they are unhappy and when they are unhappy, they cry, sulk or throw a tantrum. It is therefore up to parents to teach children how to win and lose at sport and somehow imbue them with the true Corinthian spirit. When you think about it, we are trying to get children to understand a confusing concept. 'You've got to try your best and not let the side down. If, however, your best isn't good enough then you have to pretend that you don't mind and go and shake hands cordially with someone you want to punch.'

How to Teach Children to Lose Graciously

Before the age of three, it is unrealistic to expect children to understand the complexities of losing. Once they are old enough to play competitive games, then you can introduce the concept of winning and losing. If your child is throwing tantrums when he loses, then you should begin to teach him how to lose. Play a board game or have a game of football in the garden, allow the child to win and then you can begin to model a script for good losing.

'You won! Well done! I didn't win and I feel a bit sad, but I am happy you won.'

Next time you play a game, tell him that he might lose and if he does he might feel upset. Tell him in games we can't always win, that's what makes them fun, but when we do lose we have to accept it without making a fuss. Remind him what you said when you lost last time and tell him this is what he has to say when he loses. Engineer a victory for yourself in the next game (if you are able to!) and then remind him what he has to do when he loses. Keep on acknowledging his feelings about losing and give him lots of praise. 'You wish you'd won. It can feel really annoying when you lose, can't it? But remember you have to deal with it in the right way.'

If he manages to lose well then give him loads of praise. If he throws a tantrum, try and ignore it as much as possible. Next time you play a game, do an actual rehearsal of how he will cope if he loses.

At my school, the boys come to us as terrible losers, and whenever they lose they throw an almighty strop that often ends up with them trying to attack the opposition, their own team or the referee. We spend a lot of time teaching them how to lose well and how to win graciously, and we get them to rehearse how they will behave when it happens. Losing puts their brains into reptile mode and so they tend to behave irrationally, so we give them a script they can rely on when their brain shuts down. We get them to imagine the feelings they will have when they lose, and then to act out being a good loser. We also acknowledge the fact that losing is painful and not easy to deal with.

Rehearsing losing helps children to be prepared when it inevitably happens. When they do lose well you have an opportunity to give them lots of descriptive praise. If necessary, you can back this up with a reward. The most simple and logical reward is that if they lose well, then you play another game with them. If they throw a strop, then you simply walk away. This clearly shows them that no one wants to play with bad losers and that if they don't accept defeat, then they don't get to play the game.

It is very tempting to deal with bad losers by banning them from competitive sport.

'Right! That's it! You're not doing football club again.'

This doesn't solve the problem. It simply shelves it until the next time you do allow him to play a competitive game. If he has had a major blow and made a big scene, then by all means ban him for a day or, if it is a team sport, from the next event. This sends a strong message about what you will tolerate, but next time you let him play spend a few minutes reminding him, teaching him and then rehearsing how to lose in the right way.

Televised Sport

Parents are often concerned by the behaviour their children witness from sports stars. This includes spitting, fighting, swearing, arguing with the referee and general disrespect to authority figures. It is inevitable that children will copy what they see from their heroes and supposed role models. It is hard to shield children from these images and it is better for children to see them, and then also appreciate the consequences of the behaviour. If the player kicks someone, he gets sent off.

Parents also need to explain that just because someone is really good at something they are not perfect and that they will make mistakes.

Sport and Games: A Summary

1 Learning to lose is a complicated skill. It takes time so don't expect too much, too soon.

2 Acknowledge to children that they will feel upset and angry when they lose. Be prepared to admit to having those feelings yourself.

3 Model good losing to your children.

4 Teach them how to lose, giving them a script and rehearsing it.

5 Give lots of descriptive praise when they lose well.

6 If they can lose well, offer to play another game with them, if they lose badly walk away.

7 If they have a major tantrum as a result of losing, banning them from the activity for the next session will send a strong message about how they should behave.

television, computers and video games

Let's be honest here: the main reason adults let their children watch television is because it keeps them quiet. Once children are over four they can get themselves up in the morning at a weekend, turn on the television and go for hours without bothering their parents, who can enjoy a well-earned lie-in. In the evenings, parents can be preparing tea, organising bedtime and talking on the phone without being interrupted if the children are slumped in front of the telly.

When I was a child there were two channels showing children's television from about 3.30 p.m. to 6 p.m. every evening, and that was it. There was little or no choice about television, and so parents did not have to worry too much about regulating it. Now, children can watch cartoons, play video games or play around on the computer all their waking hours and, depressingly, many do. Gone also is the communal habit of families making a date to sit round the television and watch a favourite programme together. Different members of families often go and watch their own programmes on their own television. There is also less planned watching of programmes and more browsing as people decide that they want to watch television and then search through the channels until something takes their fancy. There are also some questions about the quality of children's television programmes. Of course, there are some terrifically entertaining and educational programmes and there are some excellent dramas, but most of what is served up for children, including wall-to-wall cartoons, is rubbish.

A staggering proportion of children have televisions, video games and computers in their rooms and parents have little idea of what they watch and for how long. Sitting in front of a flickering screen has a damping-down effect on children. They become quiet and passive, they don't argue (except over what to watch) and don't need any adult attention. There is an epidemic of speech and language difficulties for children under five caused by families staring at a screen rather than speaking and listening to each other. Also, children who look at screens all day don't learn to play properly, either on their own or with their siblings and friends, and have underdeveloped social skills. Not the best start in life.

However, I think some telly is good for us and there are five good reasons for children to sit in front of a screen: relaxation, entertainment, communication, imagination and education.

How Much Telly is Okay?

Screen-time is no longer regulated by television schedules and so the responsibility has been passed on to parents as to what and how much television is appropriate for children. My own rough guide aims to balance out the entertainment, educational and super-babysitter aspects of television with the damage that too much vegetating can do. This is not meant to be a stick to beat you with and there are times when, for very good reasons, such as lie-ins after a late night, or getting organised to go on holiday, when letting your children watch for much longer is a godsend.

■ *Under threes:* Not more than twenty minutes. Let them watch one simple programme devised for this age group. It is useful to reward this as a condition of getting dressed in the morning, or getting ready for bed. Avoid programmes that are loud, have lots of busy moving images or any violence.

■ *Three to five:* Up to half an hour a day of easy-to-follow simple narrative.

■ *Five to seven:* Up to forty-five minutes a day of television or computer time. Watching simple, entertaining programmes with lots of stories and singing, or fiddling around on the computer looking at websites for books and authors they have enjoyed is fine.

■ *Seven to ten*: Up to an hour a day of computer and
television, including not more than fifteen minutes
of video games.

It is interesting to do a rough calculation of how much
television your children do watch. If it is radically more
than my guide I would suggest you reduce it. Look at
when and why your children are in front of a screen and
have a think about what they could be doing instead.
Remember, you don't have to keep your children enter-
tained all the time. It is good for them be bored and to
have to devise their own ways of keeping themselves
amused. One of the problems that is caused by television
is that it provides instant entertainment with no effort or
input from the viewer. This means children are in the
habit of passively expecting things to be laid on for them.
It is fascinating to watch what happens to children when
there are somewhere without a television, or when it
breaks. At first they wander around listlessly feeling bored
and under-stimulated. After a bit, a toy, a book or a game
grabs their attention and they are off, lost in a world
of imagination, and can play for hours. When given the
choice, children, like adults, will usually turn to the instant
entertainment and gratification of television rather than
take the trouble to play.

Get your children into the habit of turning off the television or computer when you ask them to, as a condition
of allowing them to watch or play in the first place. When
you are going to call them for tea give them a ten-minute
warning so they can get themselves geared up for turning

it off. When they are a little older, they can learn to record things if they are desperate to watch something. As adults know, videoing a programme makes missing it more tolerable, even when you know you'll probably never get round to watching it. Don't get into protracted negotiations about turning off the television. If they won't turn it off when you ask them to, then they can't watch the following day. The penny will soon drop.

Don't let children eat in front of the television even if the telly is in the kitchen. Eating together, round a table, is an important time to improve on speaking and listening and to learn good table manners. Let them have a telly tea or breakfast as a reward, once in a while. They will love it, particularly if you make a real fuss about it.

Televisions and Computers in Bedrooms

I am going to sound like a real old-stick-in-the-mud here but I don't think children should have a television in their bedroom and they should only have computers when they are being used for schoolwork. It is not possible to monitor what your child is exposed to if they have screens in their rooms and you won't be able to regulate how much they watch. Children will learn how easy it is to switch off the television or minimise their computer screen when they hear you coming. This advice may be harder to follow for people who have less space, if having the children watching television in the main living space disturbs the rest of the family. In these circumstances children could watch television in their bedroom but I would be sure that it is off when it is supposed to be. If you feel you can't trust your child to keep the television off in the evening then remove the cable from the back so they have to ask if they want to watch it. Children should not generally watch television in the hour before bed, as the flickering images over-stimulate their brains and make it harder to wind down.

Film nights (or afternoons) are a good way of giving children a treat or a reward. If they have achieved a behaviour target, or you are just feeling kind, get a DVD out, make some popcorn, draw the curtains and make it an occasion. This is a world away from your child watching nameless, random television alone in his bedroom.

Television works well as a reward. Offering the possibility of an extra twenty minutes on Friday or Saturday night can be a good target for children to work towards.

Computer Games

Older children, particularly boys, love playing these games. They can be mesmerised for hours and they are every bit as good a babysitter as a television. But apart from creating children who can use a high-tech weapons system on a modern fighter jet, video games have no benefits. There is little or no educational value, they are addictive and, most importantly, they are taking up valuable time that could be used for playing, socialising and speaking and listening. Children who spend hours on computer games have delayed speech and poor social skills. One of the most common and time-consuming things we have to do at my school is teach children who have spent their early years playing endless video games how to communicate. We also have to teach parents to play with their children and try and fill in the gaps in development that have resulted from hours spent alone in front of a screen. If you allow your child to have computer games, have strictly enforced limits of how long they can play for in a day (see above). In addition, if your child does have a computer game, it can be used as an effective reward. Time playing computer games could be linked to achieving targets or completing chores.

Gameboy or Homework Boy

I did some work with a mother whose seven-year-old son was spending two hours a day on his Gameboy. She had never really decided how much screen-time was reasonable and it had gradually grown until it was out of hand. She was shocked when I suggested we cut it down to no more than fifteen minutes a day. She said her son would never accept this and she would have a full-scale tantrum on her hands. I tactfully reminded her that she was the adult and that it was up to her what her child did and not the other way round. We compromised on twenty minutes, but we agreed to time this strictly. In addition, before her son was allowed his time, he had to complete his homework. We also got him to agree that he would turn off his game as soon as he was asked to and that any delaying would result in the time being taken off the next day's session. I also suggested she give him a two-minute warning so the ending wouldn't come as too much of a shock. On the first day he absolutely refused to turn off the Gameboy. We knew this was coming and had planned that, rather than grab it off him and have a big fight, she would take it when he had finished. She would explain that as he hadn't stopped when she had asked him, he wouldn't be getting it the following night. This didn't seem to faze him much, as he probably didn't believe her.

The next day when he asked for his Gameboy, she reminded him what had happened the day before and that, as a result, he wasn't going to be allowed a go that night. He threw a tantrum of epic proportions, screaming, shouting and trashing his bedroom. I had planned for this with his mother so she was primed to stay tough and not to give in. When he had finished, she said he would be allowed his twenty minutes the next evening if he put his bedroom back together. After a bit of huffing and puffing, he got down to it. The next day, she reminded him what would happen if he didn't stop when he was asked and gave him the Gameboy back. He got a two-minute warning and was then told it was time to stop.

'I'll just finish the stage I'm on,' he said, and played on for another three minutes before stopping. This was a considerable improvement and his mother gave him lots of praise. She said this was good enough for her and she didn't feel she needed to be any tighter.

I told her that by allowing him twenty-three minutes, when she had said it would be only twenty, she was in danger of slipping back towards square one.

Sometime later, I bumped into her and her son at the doctors' surgery. He was plugged into his Gameboy and she gave me a slightly helpless shrug. I was called in to see the doctor, and when I came out ten minutes later, the boy was still playing on his machine.

Television, Computers and Video Games: A Summary

1 Have an idea of what is a reasonable amount of screen-time for your child per day, stick to it and be firm. There are plenty of other things they can do. Being bored and having to create your own entertainment is an important part of growing up.

2 Train your children to turn off the television as soon as you ask them to.

3 Don't use television as a regular babysitting service, however peaceful it makes the house. Too much screen-time is not good for children.

4 Beware children claiming that they need to spend hours on the internet for homework. Check with the teacher and keep an eye on the websites the children are looking at.

5 Ensure you have a good firewall to protect your children from unsuitable images. My six-year-old son once innocently put Willy Wonka into Google and the result needed some tactful explanation.

6 If at all possible, don't allow televisions in bedrooms.

7 Take account of ratings of television and video games, which are there to protect your child. Don't fall for the 'My friends are all allowed to watch 18s'. First, they probably aren't, and second, even if they are it doesn't mean your children should.

conclusion

The message of this book is simple: parents spend far too much time trying to improve behaviour when they are stressed and in reptile mode. Often parents are left feeling frustrated and guilty for being so bad-tempered and there is then a danger they will over-compensate. Don't try to sort out bad behaviour when it is happening, instead, make a plan when you are calm. Focus on one thing you want to change and teach your child how you want it done. Nine times out of ten parents know where the flashpoints with behaviour are likely to be. By making a clear plan in advance you will feel calm and stay in control.

To improve your child's behaviour, use the 6 to 1 strategy. It feels strange and it takes practice, but the result will be a fundamental change in both you and your child. Getting into the habit of noticing what your child is doing right and praising him goes against the grain. We seem to be programmed to focus on the few things that are going wrong, rather than the great majority of things that are going right. Praise is the key to improving children's behaviour, it makes parenting positive and fun.

When bad behaviour has become a pattern, adding rewards and logical consequences are useful motivators. Carefully targeted rewards help the child to know exactly what is expected of him. Reward systems also help parents to stay positive and keep praising.

Children respond to clear rules and routines – they help them to feel safe in a world which can often seem scary and unpredictable. Once a routine has become ingrained then children will begin to follow it automatically, without needing to be nagged or chased.

Remember to use lots of 'panto' when dealing with behaviour. Give the behaviour you want to see the hard sell and make doing the right thing fun and exciting. Rehearsals are really effective in showing the child precisely what you expect from them. Children love doing a dry run and parents will be amazed at how well the child remembers what they are supposed to do.

I hope that as a result of reading this book, you will play more with your children. It doesn't have to be for hours, or every day. Giving your child a few minutes when they are in charge, the rules are set by them and there is no right or wrong way of doing things will have a far deeper and more powerful effect than we can imagine.

And please don't forget to praise yourself. Being a parent is hard work and we spend far too much time being critical of ourselves. Notice all the things you are doing well and give yourself a pat on the back. How about a bit of 6 to 1 for parents?

Good luck!

index

divas and dictators

Acknowledgements

I would like to thank my agent Tif Loehnis for all her encouragement and advice, Miranda West and everyone at Vermilion for their guidance, patience and support, Petra Cramsie and my wife, Lucy Taylor, for their invaluable help, and lastly my children, Ollie, Iris and Kit.